Straight Out of Barrio Hollywood

The Adventures of Telemundo Co-founder Frank H. Cruz
Chicano History Professor, TV Anchorman,
Network Executive, and Public Broadcasting Leader

Frank H. Cruz
and **Rita Joiner Soza**

outskirts press

Straight Out of Barrio Hollywood
The Adventures of Telemundo Co-founder Frank Cruz,
Chicano History Professor, TV Anchorman, Network Executive, and Public Broadcasting Leader

v6.0

Outskirts Press, Inc.
http://www.outskirtspress.com

Paperback ISBN: 978-1-9772-0517-9
Hardback ISBN: 978-1-9772-0518-6

Library of Congress Control Number: 2019900223

PRINTED IN THE UNITED STATES OF AMERICA

Author's Note

To write this book, I've relied on my memory and many interviews with family and friends. I've also consulted media coverage and books that reference some of the more noteworthy events. Overall, the work reflects my personal experience and recollection, and I have worked to make it as accurate as possible.

Frank H. Cruz

His memoir is Frank Cruz' second book. He co-authored one of the first secondary education textbooks on Latin American civilization while teaching high school and college history classes. Cruz was the first Chicano reporter to be assigned to cover strictly Latino issues for television for which he earned Emmy and Golden Mike Awards. That career lead Cruz and a partner to develop and operate the second Spanish-language television station in Los Angeles. Their success with KVEA-TV was the first step in building the coast-to-coast network Telemundo. Later Cruz and another partner started the nation's first Latino-owned life insurance company. His business acumen and broadcast experience lead Cruz to be appointed to the Corporation for Public Broadcasting, where he served for 13 years. Cruz is a trustee of University of Southern California, a director of Latino Public Broadcasting, and a former director of The Irvine Foundation. Cruz earned a master's degree in history from USC. He lives in Southern California with his wife Bonnie and near his three children and their families.

Other titles by Cruz:

The Latin Americans Past and Present (1972)

Rita Joiner Soza

This is Soza's second book. She is a retired business professor and a former Fortune 100 human resources executive. Soza is a second-generation Los Angeles native. She grew up in Montebello, California, and earned an MBA degree from University of California at Irvine. She lives in San Diego County with her husband Geoff and spends a good deal of time in Los Angeles visiting her daughter and school chums and working on various writing projects.

Other titles by Soza:

> *Helen Miller Bailey: The Pioneer Educator and Renaissance Woman Who Shaped Chicano Leaders* (2015)

Table of Contents

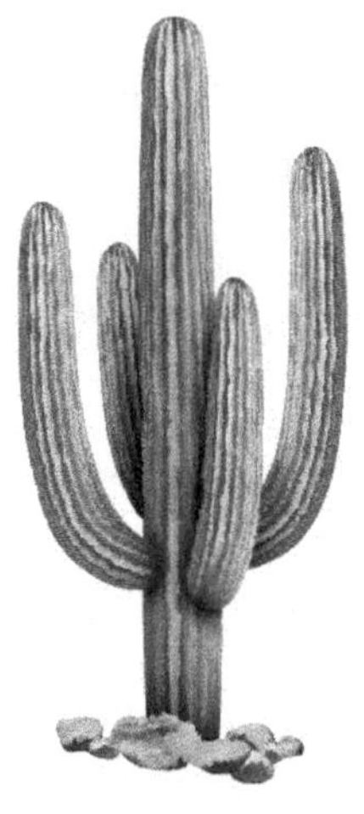

Part I

Part II

Part III

Foreword

The United States' mid-term election of 2018, if nothing else, clearly demonstrated that the Hispanic electorate is a force to be reckoned with. Not only did we awaken to our own power and offer a host of candidates, but the powerful have realized that we can no longer be marginalized or ignored, since we were a deciding factor in several important races. That indomitable Latino spirit is celebrated in this memoir of the trailblazing, multi-faceted career of educator, author, journalist, and business executive Frank Cruz.

I first knew of Frank in the early 1970s, when he was a young Chicano reporter for KABC-TV, Channel 7, in Los Angeles. He often reported on the political career of my father, Congressman Edward Roybal. During those years, there was an absence of Latino reporters, and it was helpful and inspiring to me as a young Chicana to see someone on television who looked like my family and my classmates talking about issues important to our neighborhoods.

For those raised in the Chicano culture, and especially for today's younger generation, Frank's memoir opens a very personal window that illuminates the struggles and challenges faced by our early leaders who aimed to honor our ancient history by taking a rightful place in politics, education, business, or public service and who opened doors for those of us who followed. On many occasions, I have heard Frank denounce what he called "second-class citizenship" for Chicanos. To that end, his memoir describes the personal risk-taking that has been required and supported by optimism rooted in the knowledge of our ancestral accomplishments.

For those who seek to increase their personal or institutional cultural competency, Frank's stories, told with humor and authenticity, offer steps toward a truly empathetic understanding of people of color and "others" who seek only a level playing field on which to pursue the American dream.

For young people of any background, Frank provides a model of how a young person can assemble the wisdom, transferrable expertise, and problem-solving skills which will surely be needed in their life – a life which economists predict will require multiple and diverse career changes, rather than a predictable progression in a single field. Frank also provides a model of how personal success can be used to empower underserved individuals and communities.

And finally, business educators and professionals who understand the value of entrepreneurship to the local and global economy will enjoy Frank's unique documentation of the development of the media in the United States, and how the industry has been shaped to meet societal needs, if not demands. For example, Frank tells the story of how he and his partner Joe Wallach (and a giant debt) built the Telemundo coast-to-coast network of television stations and production facilities in less than one year – an important case study in market leadership.

Having known Frank Cruz for decades, and having followed his impactful career, I can testify that he has always been at the forefront of the struggle for justice and understanding for Latinos, and that he has taken barrier-breaking risks to make America a more inclusive and culturally expansive society. His book vividly captures the times and events that have shaped his multiple pinnacle careers and brought Latinos to our present tipping point, where it is neither possible to discount our influence culturally, nor to ignore our participation politically.

United States Congresswoman Lucille Roybal-Allard

Introduction

Over the years, friends and colleagues have often encouraged me to document my many years in broadcasting, which include introducing groundbreaking, industry milestones, somewhat remarkable in those early days for a brown man in a white world. Also lingering has been my personal desire to tell the story of assembling the second Spanish-language, coast-to-coast television network in the United States in less than one year—telling the story of Telemundo, if you will.

It was my co-author, Rita Joiner Soza, who first offered to work with me on a memoir. We became friends while Rita was writing the biography of a professor at East Los Angeles College whose history classes had been inspiring to both of us. Rita helped me get over some reservations I had about telling my story.

I ran the idea of a memoir by numerous Chicano leaders and historians. They indicated that much has been written on the issues of second-class citizenship of Latinos in the United States. In their words, from a historical perspective, we know a lot about the 1968 East Los Angeles Walkouts and more broadly about the Chicano Movement of the sixties and seventies. What my colleagues insisted was that, though events have been covered, "sadly, we don't know much about the individual Latino activists." They said things like, "Frank, your story and that of others are exactly what is needed to round out the history. Much has been written and presented in film about César Chávez and Dolores Huerta, but that's about it."

Rita and other colleagues were right. I agreed that the time was right to put something down on paper. Once I got over an initial hesitation, she and I became engaged in the project.

I'm not one to ruminate on, or second-guess, my motivations, but as I look back on the last 50 years, and even now with this project, I clearly see that throughout my career my purpose has been to provide knowledge to and about the Latino community in the hope of correcting misinformation and defying injustice. That passion has propelled me through several successful leadership roles.

The individual stories came easy. I am a historian and names, dates, details, and cultural context flowed effortlessly to my notepad. I had a history professor at the University of Southern California who said that history is like pulling at a thread of a knitted sweater. You pull and pull and, eventually and slowly, you get back to where the sweater began. That image served me well over the years, and I have tried to apply it again as I reflect on my half century of work in education, television reporting, and network management.

My love of history was kindled by Latin American scholar Professor Helen Miller Bailey, who was teaching that subject long before academia considered it relevant. Together we authored a textbook I used while I was the Chicano Studies department chair at California State University at Long Beach.

In 1969, my work was recognized along with other professors when we were asked by KNBC-TV in Los Angeles to produce a 20-segment, Chicano heritage television show. I hosted each segment as well as contributed lectures on the Mexican War and immigration issues.

That groundbreaking series was seen by the Los Angeles news director at KABC-TV who hired me to report on the Hispanic community in Southern California. The opportunity was a challenge and an honor I couldn't pass up. Prior to 1970, we had only a handful of Latinos working in journalism, and none to my knowledge had been hired in broadcasting to focus solely on topics relevant to our unique issues. Rubén Salazar had that beat at the *Los Angeles Times* throughout the 1960s.

Just a few years later, I was offered the weekend anchor spot at KNBC-TV, which afforded me more resources as a reporter and where I began my education in the business of television production over the next ten years.

All that experience and the broad, personal and professional network I developed over the years laid the groundwork to co-own and operate the second Spanish-language television station in Los Angeles. Managing KVEA-TV set the stage for leading a small team, alongside Joe Wallach (and a gigantic loan), to assemble Telemundo, America's second Spanish-language television network. The zeal with which we approached this massive project was fueled by our shared passion to offer quality news and information to the Hispanic community.

That experience in broadcasting was then recognized by President Bill Clinton who appointed me to the Corporation for Public Broadcasting (CPB) where I served for 12 years. Indeed, I was the first minority to serve as CPB's chair person. I'm proud that many groundbreaking programs were produced during my leadership at CPB, such as *American Family* and *Maya and Miguel*.

Today, I serve as a trustee of the University of Southern California and as a director of Latino Public Broadcasting. When called to speak on behalf of these organizations, I often augment the desired topic with scenarios that have formed the basis for this book.

I hope readers, especially young Latinos and Latinas looking to succeed as educators, journalists, scientists, business professionals, or as political leaders, will find my story helpful in navigating a path to fulfillment of their passions through careers in our high-tech, globally competitive environment. The key is acknowledging and developing the building blocks that advance a successful person from one level to the next. I must admit—a little luck doesn't hurt either.

The more I think about the concept of "building blocks," I can't help but conjure up images of Aztec and Mayan pyramids. I can't imagine how I broke down so many barriers by any other means than by building on sets of events and learning experiences. I cultivated varied expertise and took a lot of risks. All of this was mortared together with authentic relationship-building in support of the plan, my guiding purpose, my passion.

My memoir attempts to detail the contents of these building blocks and how they came to be placed. While this is, of course, my life's path, it seems worthwhile that another person might look at such a model and consider the blocks they are constructing and consider those that might need to be developed or strengthened. Individuals will need to determine for themselves what they use for their mortar. What is their passion; what is their life's purpose?

Engage Service
Establish Expertise
Accumulate Assets
Nurture Relationships
Devour Education & Travel
Establish Work Ethic

Prologue

The Corporation for Public Broadcasting on Trial

Preparing to testify before a congressional committee requires extensive preparation by a whole team. As chairman of the board of directors for the Corporation for Public Broadcasting (CPB) from 1999 through 2001, I took the lead of that process prior to each of my several visits to Congress. However, never had it been more critical to effectively communicate the value of public broadcasting to the American people than in 1996, when the future of the CPB in the United States was on trial. As the chair of CPB, the threat was both national and personal.

The grandeur of the setting, the photographers squatting on the ground at your feet to get a unique shot, and the unwelcoming glares from many of the congressional panel, all elevated the apprehension of the proceedings. But during my 15 years as a news reporter, I had become well-acquainted with the high drama and high stakes atmosphere of a federal hearing.

The Corporation for Public Broadcasting funds 1,600 public television and radio stations around the county, with a combined viewer and listenership of more than 100 million. In fact, 99 percent of U.S. households have access to public radio and television. In many rural areas, public broadcasting has been the only source of balanced local, national, and world news since established by Congress in 1967. Millions in these small towns and farming communities could have lost virtually all access to current events had I been unable to provide indisputable and compelling testimony as to the system's value.

The criticism was that public broadcasting news programs were biased in favor of a liberal viewpoint. This perspective completely disregarded the fact that Public Broadcasting Service (PBS) television and National Public Radio (NPR) journalists always make a valiant attempt to present both sides of any issue. Not every newsmaker is keen on speaking to a true investigative reporter, or a person may truly be unavailable for comment, thus, not all positions on the topic can be reported. Such frequent outcomes can misleadingly be provided as evidence that public broadcasting is slanted.

The Speaker and His Contract with Which America?

My own life's work to educate and inspire underserved people with thorough and accessible local, national, and international news coverage was under attack—the charge led by then Speaker of the House Newt Gingrich. The speaker used two tools to undermine the credibility of public broadcasting: (1) the media and (2) technology.

The Media

Throughout the 1980s, U.S. courts had been striking blows against the "Fairness Doctrine," which, since 1949, had required television and radio station license holders, to attempt anyway, to broadcast proponent and opponent viewpoints regarding any matters of public importance. The result of various court findings against what was deemed an "intrusion by the government on journalistic freedom," was that by 1987, the Federal Communications Commission (FCC) was, sadly, no longer defending or enforcing the Fairness Doctrine.

A decade later, the Telecommunications Act of 1996 and subsequent FCC-published Broadcast Ownership Rules required the deregulation, indeed the complete elimination, of restrictions on the number of radio and television licenses (stations) that a single entity could control nationwide. The operating premise was, especially in the case of radio stations (which were experiencing financial problems during the 1990s), that if an entity could own more stations it could capitalize on the greater advertising sales revenue and lower its expenses by taking advantage of the synergies existing among those various stations. For example, one advertising sales person could serve five stations. The deregulation presumption was that as radio broadcasting returned to a profitable venture, the public would benefit by a greater number of stations and thus a greater diversity of content. Well, it just didn't work out that way.

The decomposing of the Fairness Doctrine and the deregulation of station ownership laid fertile ground for the number of right-wing hate speech radio shows to mushroom and intoxicate huge audiences through national syndication. Overnight, the likes of Rush Limbaugh, Mike Savage, and Glenn Beck became national figures. In fact, a 1998 Loyola Marymount University and Loyola Law School report stated the existence of "compelling evidence that radio deregulation has resulted in great harm to public interest, such as the lack of diversity, of localism, and of competition in radio."

In addition to the string of legal findings, the FCC's own Local Radio Station Ownership Rules congealed with its Newspaper/Broadcast Cross-Ownership Ban and the agency's data collection process to establish a "diversity index." The broadcast industry had become a complex mass of legal-speak. Just so we could get our arms around the dynamic and immense changes in the industry during the 1990s, we had to invite a legal historian to present the timeline and varying legal rationales to the CPB board members.

Conservative politicians, in particular House Speaker Gingrich, used their invitations to be interviewed on these nationally syndicated, angry radio shows to spread the philosophy that the U.S. government had no role in funding television and radio. Gingrich repeatedly made the commitment to his radio audiences that he was going to "rid the country of public broadcasting altogether."

Technology

Since March of 1979, cable and satellite television companies had funded a new television network called C-SPAN (Cable-Satellite Public Affairs Network) as a public service, purportedly designed to increase political literacy across the nation. Often during the 1990s, a C-SPAN camera was fixed on the floor of the House of Representatives. Speaker Gingrich found that he could sit literally on the floor of Congress, directly in front of the C-SPAN camera, and viewers could see only his face on their television screens. This positioning gave the appearance that the room must have otherwise been filled with congressional representatives listening intently to Gingrich. Rather, he would engage in these tirades entirely alone in the chambers. He would literally carry on for hours describing his "Contract with America," which did not contain a line item for public broadcasting.

Mainstream use of the Internet was also taking off in the 1990s, providing platforms for extremists on both ends of the political scene to spew vitriol while remaining somewhat obscure and "under the radar." One of the firsts to make a national name for himself via his email service was Matt Drudge and his *Drudge Report.* Initially reporting on entertainment and political gossip, Drudge reportedly got a tip that a *Newsweek* reporter was sitting on a story about President Bill Clinton and a White House intern named Monica Lewinski. Emailing information, on what was to become a major scandal, to his audience list of about one thousand made Drudge a national figure and certainly contributed to Clinton being impeached for perjury and obstruction of justice in 1998. To highlight how profitable the Internet became early on for otherwise unknown individuals, by 2003 Drudge was reporting some $1.2 million a year in advertising revenue.

Little doubt exists that these technological advances have had a causal relationship with the political polarization of our government officials and our citizenry.

Budget Hawks

The assault on public broadcasting didn't just emanate from the floor of the House and the angry voices of the likes of Drudge, Beck, Limbaugh, and Savage. Although the federal budget was nearly balanced in 1995, followed by annual surpluses during the next four years of Bill Clinton's presidency, I sat in that federal hearing facing conservative budget hawks, who, with a majority in Congress, were sensing the opportunity to defund or degrade social-service programs. Administrators of Medicare, Medicaid, and Aid to Families with Dependent Children were all facing the same tough questioning as I was. We were all reporting on the efficiencies of our programs and justifying our very existence. Some programs lost funding and some emerged unscathed. As often is the case, when social programs are attacked, the most powerless among us are the victims.

To understand the public broadcasting system, it is important to understand the funding mechanisms. The federal financial budgeting process works like this: the administration makes its request for funding all aspects of government spending, and then the House and Senate set their individual appropriation levels. In the end, a final federal budget is negotiated and approved, except when it isn't approved, and a government shutdown is the painful result.

Appropriation for CPB is included for each of the following two budgetary years. These appropriations represent approximately 15 percent of the overall costs for all public television and radio stations, with some outlets receiving more federal funding than others. The remainder of the public broadcasting system's budget comes from individual families, private foundations, and state and local grants. The importance of available, local funding sources cannot be overstated. Although in a few of the largest urban centers, public broadcasting might survive without federal money, the bulk of operation costs in rural areas and mid-sized markets are covered by congressional appropriation.

Congressional appropriations had been steadily increased in federal budgets, nearly every year since the CPB was established in 1967. The conservatives in Congress had their way, however, in the five years between 1994 and 1999, when funding was decreased each of those years. In 1996, the situation was particularly frustrating because CPB was concluding plans for the extraordinary transformation of all public television stations from analog signals to digital transmission, as prescribed by the Federal Telecommunications Act of 1996.

In 1994 and 1995, the Clinton administration had shepherded the technology conversion discussions that became law in 1996. The agreement on precisely how the law would be implemented was nicknamed "the Grand Alliance." It was an appropriately lofty title for an event that affected literally every household in the United States, and yet it remains an accomplishment that is wholly unknown to the average television viewer.

The Telecommunications Act of 1996 established the last year that repair parts could be sold for analog television sets, the last year the sets themselves could be manufactured and sold, and the last dates that analog signals would be allowed to be broadcast in the United States. For the first time, and seemingly unlikely to be repeated, an entire industry and all government-related entities had agreed on something. This included the Clinton administration, both houses of Congress, television broadcasters, television network owners, television set manufacturers, and television broadcasting equipment manufacturers.

Technology advances and the U.S. competitive spirit had coalesced to prevent Japanese and German scientists and their respective television industries from setting the worldwide High Definition (HDTV) broadcast standards for the eminent transition to digital transmission from analog in the mid-nineties.

Digital transmission started first in the major markets—New York, Chicago, Los Angeles—due to the costly conversion expense of $2 to $5 million for each station. These networks and independent station owners in the largest U.S cities were deemed to have more resources to make the expensive transition to all digital equipment in their stations. Imagine, if you will, every camera, microphone, headset, and transmission tower had to be replaced; nothing could be repurposed for the new technology.

In the end, the expensive transformation was a benefit to all parties. Each station gained as much as five times spectrum wave power, providing multiple signals from which it could broadcast. For example, the ABC affiliate station in Los Angeles and independently owned KTLA could each maintain its current programming and add a channel focusing on health, sports, cooking or maybe a channel exclusively for children's programming—five additional channels in all.

The viewing audiences gained a much higher picture quality with the ability to split screens and watch multiple shows (often sports programs) at once. Also, the scroll of breaking news or other information could now be streamed along the bottom of the picture—the now-familiar crawler or news ticker.

Ultimately, very few stations, if any, took advantage of that expansion of spectrum wave power, because with each additional signal broadcast, the quality of the transmission degraded somewhat. But even the quality of a fifth signal was far superior to the old analog picture. Once viewers became accustomed to the enhanced digital picture it would prove difficult to reduce the quality. Truth be told, the stations and advertisers never really figured out how to monetize the additional programming for those channels.

In exchange for this increased spectrum power, the Clinton administration decided it was only appropriate that public interest obligations be revised. The president appointed a representative group of 21 industry leaders to recommend new FCC standards.

I was vice chair of CPB's board at that time. In addition to my number one priority of overseeing the digital conversion of 354 public television stations across the United States, President Clinton appointed me to the Advisory Committee on Public Interest Obligations of Digital Television Broadcasters, almost always referred to as the Gore Commission. The industry group, headed by Vice President Al Gore, was tasked with revising the requirements for each station to broadcast information relevant to all its viewers in addition to its commercial programming. We issued our report in December 1998.

Thus, it seemed a wicked twist of events when I found myself seated before Congress pleading for the very existence of public broadcasting. It was a responsibility I did not take lightly; indeed, my life's work had led me to that day.

But in the fall of 1996, as I faced the congressional committee in defense of CPB as its chair, I could not help but wonder if my life's experiences showed: my upbringing in a barrio, the heckling I had endured in the newsroom as one of the first Latino television reporters, or the fact that I have always thought of myself as just a simple teacher of the Chicano experience.

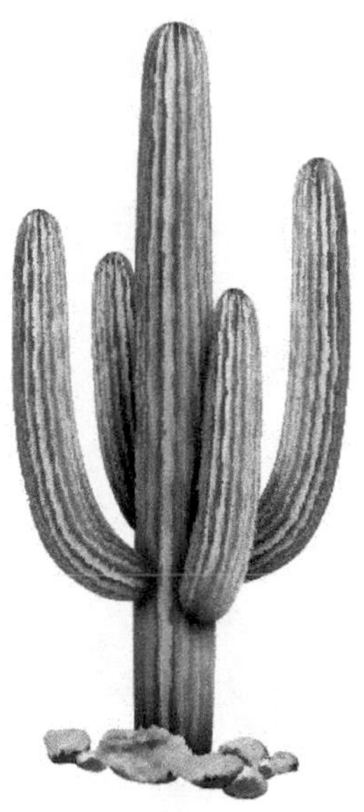

Part I

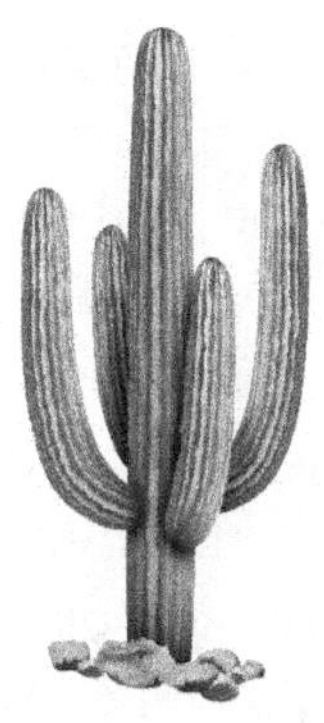

Chapter One

My Career in the Media Started in Hollywood, Barrio Hollywood, That Is

Washington D.C. is worlds away from my home town. Not just a few times throughout my career did that little voice inside my head (my inner critic) speak out, "You're a fraud, Cruz. You're a poor boy from the barrio, what do you think you are doing here?"

I was born in the Tucson, Arizona, neighborhood called Barrio Hollywood. The small cluster of homes and a few small businesses just six blocks north to south and eight blocks east to west is bordered on the east by the Santa Cruz River. Not until I put pen to paper to begin this book did it occur to me that our family name was the same as the river that kept all of us at arms-length from the English-speaking residents of Tucson.

The Mexican Revolution began in 1910 and didn't end until 1920/21. My mother's father, Rosendo Osuna, had survived as a landholder by the end of the war, but the fighting to protect his land had become quite dangerous for his family of six girls and two boys. So, my grandfather brought the five younger girls up to Nogales, Arizona, to live with their oldest sister, Ernestine, who had married and lived there with her husband, Mr. Valencia. My mother and her four other sisters ranged in age from 6 to 12. Their brothers, my uncles, stayed in México with Grandpa Osuna. Eventually, a second sister got married and the four unmarried sisters followed her to Tucson.

Grandad Osuna with his daughter, my mom, Rutília "Ruth" Osuna Cruz

Later, the youngest daughter, my aunt Consuelo "Connie" moved west to San Diego and then on to East Los Angeles. Many years later, after leaving the U.S. Air Force, I would live with my Aunt Connie and her husband and begin my academic career in Los Angeles.

My father's family was part of the rich silver and copper mining history in Chihuahua, México. Just as with every other major economic boom in America, such as agriculture and railroad construction, copper mining was another economic pull factor. Consequently, my dad's family followed the mining jobs, ending up in Tucson.

There has never been enough of a labor pool in the United States to satisfy the needs of industry. For example, here in the West, our farmers feed the country but have never had enough local people to work the fields, thus, migrant farmworkers follow the ripening of the crops all up and down California. After the Korean Conflict we had an explosion of infrastructure construction projects with a meager pool of qualified workers. And today, our high-tech companies experience the same challenges due to the lack of available H1B Visas for needed foreign workers.

The Osuna and Cruz families were part of the growth of Barrio Hollywood in the late 1930s and early 1940s as a logical place for working families to settle. My parents met on the job at the Tucson Laundry owned by Oliver Drachman. My mom worked the machines and my dad drove one of the delivery trucks. These hard-working young people, together with my aunt Gaudelia "Delia" purchased land in the barrio (nearly the whole block) along St. Mary's Road up to the corner of Columbia Avenue in Tucson.

My older brother, Richard "Dickie," was born soon after my parents' marriage. Sadly, when Mom was pregnant with me three years later, Dad contracted meningitis and died very quickly after slipping into a coma that summer. Moses Cruz was born that October 4 of 1939. Yes, had it not been for the cajoling of my dear aunts Delia and Connie, Mom would have burdened a little boy with a larger than life name. As it happened, she acquiesced, and Frank Cruz got to grow up setting my own expectations for myself and living free from any comparisons to a Biblical icon.

Aunt Gaudelia "Delia" and Grandad Osuna with my older brother Richard "Dickie" and me

Mom with Dickie and me

My mom was just 24 years old with two boys and a low-paying job that required her to be away from home several hours a day. Somehow, she gathered the courage and the money to convert one of the houses on Columbia Avenue to the Columbia Café (the three of us lived in the house next door to the café). To prepare for the opening of her restaurant she had to learn the local and more popular Sonora-style cooking, because she was raised in Sinaloa where fish is a main recipe ingredient.

Dressed for my First Holy Communion

Fortunately for me, although I never knew my father, my mom was a very powerful role model. Mom's entrepreneurial spirit and that of the many hardworking folks of Barrio Hollywood is certainly a big part of who I am.

Over the years I've heard two different, both plausible, explanations for naming our poor Tucson neighborhood Barrio Hollywood.

A short drive west along West Speedway Road, the northern border of Barrio Hollywood, takes the visitor directly to the Old Tucson Studios, where some 400 films and other commercial productions have been shot. Labelling a nearby barrio after the film capital of the world doesn't seem like too much of a stretch.

However, when I scanned a list of the films shot at the Tucson location, I only found three that were old enough to have caused the neighborhood to be so christened, early on: *Reunification* in 1910, *Ridin' Wild* in 1925, and *A Son of His Father* in 1925. Whereas in the fifties, iconic Westerns such as *Rio Bravo* and *Gunfight at OK Corral* preceded *Cimarron* in the sixties along with the popular television series, *Broken Arrow*. In the seventies, *Outlaw Josey Wales*, *Easy Rider*, *How the West was Won*, *McLintock!*, and later *Wild, Wild West*, were all filmed just west of Tucson. Because, as far as I can tell, most of the filming was done well after Barrio Hollywood got its name, the next story gets my vote as the more likely accurate account.

The second theory or popular legend requires a bit of meteorological preface. The weather pattern in Tucson is similar to conditions in the Mexican states of Sinaloa and Chihuahua from where my mother's and father's families, respectively, escaped the chaos of a post-Revolution México.

In the United States, Arizona is part of the North American Monsoon Region, which includes the Santa Catalina Mountains. Continuing southward and into México the region includes the Sierra Madre Occidental in the states of Sinaloa, Chihuahua, Durango, and Sonora. As summer reaches its peak in mid-June, the entire monsoon region experiences a mix of high temperature, high winds, and high humidity. These conditions bring on monsoon thunderstorms, that drop nearly half the region's annual rainfall in just 30 days. From mid-July to mid-August storms drench the entire area, just when the temperatures reach an unbearable crescendo.

Throughout my growing up (and still in some areas) there were no paved streets in Barrio Hollywood and no flood control infrastructure. So, the monsoon storms' short, but heavy, downpours created giant mud puddles in our streets, in our backyards, on the paths we used to walk to school, and in the many gullies around town.

Dickie and me on the dirt streets of Barrio Hollywood

Usually, at this point when explaining my roots to a new business acquaintance or to an inquisitive student, most people remain at a loss to see the connection to their inevitable question, "So why do they call it Barrio Hollywood?" I then explain that those puddles, large or small, became swimming holes, of sorts, for the kids of the barrio. We had all seen the movies that suggested that every home in Hollywood, California, had a swimming pool in the backyard. So, you see, for those couple of months each summer, all over town were dozens of versions of a swimming pool—thus the name Barrio Hollywood.

Regardless of how the neighborhood was christened, I did get my start in the media—radio reporting to be exact—in Barrio Hollywood. Glenwood Broyles was the teacher of a radio class at Tucson High School. Why I took his class, I don't know. We did have a radio at home, in fact I have it in my home now in California, but back then I don't remember having a particular interest in radio programs. We had no television and did not get a telephone in the house until 1957, my last year of high school. Instead, we focused on doing our homework and all the other work necessary to keep our little family of three together.

I don't recollect much of the details either, but apparently classmate Gloria Reynaga and I met with Ernesto Portillo Sr., the manager of the first full-time Spanish-language radio station in Tucson. We convinced him to facilitate a class project we wanted to take on. Gloria and I put together a radio show. We did a half-hour broadcast in Spanish every Saturday for the full school year 1956/57.

Gloria and I would collect stories all week about the goings on at our high school. I'd get up early every Saturday morning and write my script. Then I would walk over to Gloria's house, so we could walk to the station together. Gloria covered student events like club meetings, excursions, scholarship announcements and college acceptance letters. She also provided information about upcoming cultural events, such as dances and holiday celebrations. I recounted all the high school varsity and junior varsity sports teams' statistics. We reported on anything that was of interest to each other, our classmates, and our families.

Today it is difficult to imagine two reporters carrying on without guests or talking heads for nearly 30 minutes straight. But it was an exciting year that stretched our communication skills and our self-images. Gloria Reynaga and I have remained friends for all these years. She and her husband live in the Santa Catalina foothills with a beautiful view of Tucson.

It has always been clear to me that the hard circumstances of my boyhood could have resulted in a more typical barrio story of lost hope and squandered potential. But I was fortunate to have many guides and mentors throughout my life. Specifically, looking back on those early years, I realize that teacher Broyles, Station Manager Ernesto Portillo Sr., and my first media co-host, Gloria Reynaga, were pivotal figures in my development along a positive path.

Although Mom didn't pick up English until much, much later, she was a serious disciplinarian, especially when it came to homework. Consequently, I was a good student and devoted to my teachers. In junior high school I won a history award with classmate Eva Wells. As I look back, I see that my childhood interest and accomplishments in radio and history foreshadowed my future careers.

In addition to Mom's high expectations of our school work, Richard and I always kept busy with odd jobs and helping her at the Columbia Café. We also worked at the dance hall across the street from Mom's restaurant. My brother and I would clean up the place and they would give us a soda. Often my brother would show off my memorization skills, "Frankie, tell them the line-up for the Brooklyn Dodgers." I guess they got a kick out of me.

In retrospect, I can see the foundation was set for a lifetime of service, enhanced by an entrepreneurial drive. Mom had instilled a work ethic that developed my self-confidence as a high achiever at school. My brother had provided many opportunities for me to take center stage, surely in part why lecturing as a professor and on-camera TV reporting came somewhat easily. And in some strange way, I believe not having a father allowed me the freedom to create my own path, whereas I might have been expected to follow in his footsteps, live up to his expectations, maybe have even been encouraged to pursue his dreams. Instead, I became my own man.

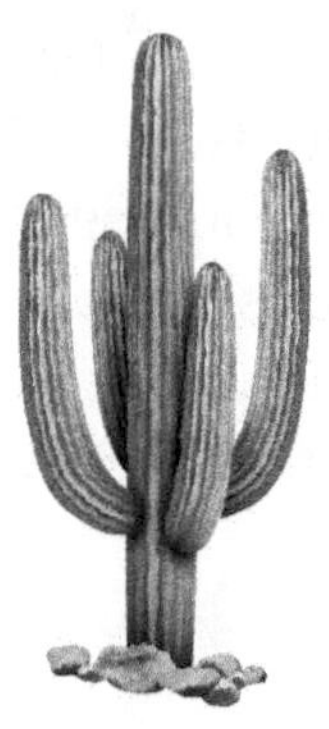

Chapter Two

Pass the Tortillas, Please

My brother and I were the principal employees of Mom's Columbia Café. Dickie was four years older than I, which would have made me about 11 or 12 years old in 1951 when he started driving us to the butcher shop where we purchased the very heavy beef stomachs that we had to scrape clean to form the basic ingredient of menudo. Maybe because he was older and truly understood the vulgarity of our task, my brother was never seen eating a bowl of that soup.

I'm not sure which aspect of my job at Columbia Café was more unpleasant—cleaning dead cows' stomach linings or waiting tables for early morning customers in dire need of a hearty bowl of menudo to face the day after a late night of tequila and beer chasers. I'm more surprised than anyone that I still love the stuff, knowing the ingredients as I do, literally, first hand.

The food at Columbia Café was very good and the place was popular. That meant that the three of us had to work very hard to maintain Mom's success. On the weekends my mother, brother, and I worked until two or three o'clock in the morning. My mother had no previous experience in the restaurant or hospitality industry, but she was such a serious and an extremely organized person that she was able to support herself and two growing boys with her small establishment.

Columbia Café

Many years later, I asked Mom why she never remarried until after Dicky and I left home. She had been, after all, a very young and very attractive widow. I'm sure she had many opportunities to date or at least go out with her sisters to a dance. But, as far as I know, she never engaged in any activities that other young people in Barrio Hollywood would have considered fun. Mom's answer was, as usual, a clear, direct, and quick response, "I didn't want any other man raising you and your brother." I knew we wouldn't speak of her decision again. That's the way it was with Mom. Tell it like it is and move on.

Many of our customers at Columbia Café were veterans of either World War II or the Korean Conflict. Late at night on the weekends I would listen to their war stories. The later the night, the more heroic warriors they became, and the more loyal to their branch of the service. Fierce fighting often broke out in the dirt in front of our café between World War II veterans and those recently returned from Korea. Each band of brothers claimed to be stronger, braver, and tougher than the other.

While I remember being frightened by their brawls, in reflection I can't help but recognize that their display of machismo influenced me. Since I had never known my father, who I noted earlier died tragically of meningitis a few months before I was born, it is likely that these "tough guys," who had served their country and lived to brag and fight about it, were role models of sorts.

What I know for sure is that I joined the United States Air Force after graduating from high school at the age of 17 and left the world in which I had been born.

I was the only guy who looked like me on that long bus ride from Tucson, Arizona, to Lackland Air Force Base in San Antonio, Texas. I have often described Barrio Hollywood as a cocoon. I had been wrapped in a safe, predictable, brown world. But the other recruits were black, white, and Asian from places like Tennessee, Wisconsin, and Oregon. They didn't look like anyone I had ever known, and they sure didn't sound like anyone I knew.

We arrived at Lackland late in the evening and were taken straight to the mess hall where we were told to grab a tray and allowed to choose any foods that appealed to us and pass on any others. This should have been easy, as we were all very hungry after the long bus ride. I guess it was easy for some; but for me, it was mind blowing. I did not see one item warming on the steam trays that I recognized.

Confused and hungry, I was so happy when I finally spied a huge stack of tortillas at the end of the line. They looked so good. I pushed my tray past others and finally at end of the line, I asked to be served some. The cook likely noticed that my plate was empty, and he piled them high. I never knew if he had also noted that my request had been to, "Pass the tortillas, please." But then he shocked me by pouring what seemed like a whole bottle of syrup over the top of my beautiful tortillas! "*Hombre, ¿qué estás pensando?*" "Man, what are you thinking?" I exclaimed.

I had never seen a pancake.

In fact, I had never actually seen any Anglo food! That late-night breakfast was the first of many culture shocks I would encounter beyond the unpaved streets of Barrio Hollywood.

Immediately upon completion of basic training and specialized courses in military police officer duties in 1957, I guess you could say I totally and literally emerged from my cocoon. My first flight was more than 15 hours long from Travis Air Force Base in Fairfield, California, to Clark Air Force Base on Luzon Island, the Philippines. After that first flight, I flew often since much of my four years as an Air Force military police officer involved safeguarding persons, valuable assets, or documents in and around the Pacific. In addition to the Philippines, I served in Japan and in Taiwan during the high stakes Taiwan Strait Crisis of 1958.

China, our ally against the Japanese in World War II, had undergone a transformation that culminated in Mao Tse-tung's Communist Party overthrowing the Chinese Nationalist Party in 1949. Chiang Kai-shek, who had led the country since 1928, retreated to the island of Taiwan located just 100 miles off the Chinese mainland with more than one million of his loyalists. They established on the island, what they claimed to be, the one, legitimate Chinese government. And it was recognized as such by the governments of the western world until Chiang Kai-shek's death in 1975.

By 1958, mainland China and its communist leaders had become emboldened by the support of the Union of Soviet Socialist Republics (USSR) and the Mikoyan (MiG) fighter jets it had deployed to the area. The decade-old People's Republic of China could have easily overtaken the small island of Taiwan and Chiang Kai-shek's tiny army. But bombing Taiwan would have caused the United States to defend its democratic ally in accordance with the Sino-American Mutual Defense Treaty that was signed in 1954. Chairman Mao instead began a provocative bombing campaign. The disputed islands in the Strait of Taiwan between the two Chinas were the targets of the borrowed MiG fighter jets.

U.S. Air Force policeman Frank Cruz

Chiang Kai-shek's Chinese Nationalists in Taiwan had U.S.-supplied, secondhand Republic F-84 Thunderjet turbojet fighter-bombers (F-84s) to fend off the communist air strikes. But the old planes, which were relics of the Korean Conflict, had, even then, been plagued by structural and engine problems.

They were no match for the Russian MiGs. The F84s were being blown out of the sky. So, the United States transported a squadron of F-104 Starfighter jets from Hamilton Air Force Base in Novato, California, and parked them on the island just north of Taiwan's capital, Taipei City.

F-104 Starfighter Jet

The F-104 jets were the first to fly at twice the speed of sound, hence the nickname "missile with a man in it." In a turnabout of fortune, the MiGs were then no match for our jets. The F-104 pilots flew their sorties at night and one of my jobs was to guard and protect the planes once they landed around 2:00 a.m. As I look back on the assignment, which at the time I considered boring and a waste of my training, I realized these fighter jets ended what could have been the first nuclear conflict of the Cold War. Although China did not possess nuclear weapons until 1964, the real issue for the United States was the spread of communism throughout Asia, which suited the ambitions of the only other nuclear power, the USSR.

At that time, however, this international intrigue was far from my consciousness. I needed to find a way to make this guard duty assignment much more palatable (foreshadowing pun intended). Evidently, worried that the U.S. government would not provide me with ample sustenance, my mom routinely sent me handmade tortillas along with containers of refried beans. (A distinct advantage of serving in the Air Force was receiving packages from home with speed on par with Fed Ex deliveries today.) I figured out that I could prepare burritos and wrap them in aluminum foil and share them with my Air Force buddies Mitch "Mike" Adler, Jimmy Quatróne, both from California, and George Rosas from Texas. I could also take the little foil-wrapped gifts from home on my middle-of-the-night guard duty; after all, I had been trained to conceal, protect, and deliver high-value items.

So, the F-104s would land while it was still dark, and the pilots would park on the flight line in preparation for daylight and the maintenance crew's work. From my guard post, I was close enough to reach out and touch the intake manifolds and the jet engines' after burners. Both were hotter than hell and perfect warming plates for my burritos. I set them down for a minute, turned them over once, and they were just like hot off the griddle at the Columbia Café.

Throughout my life I've been first in many successful endeavors, most of which involved a substantial risk to my career and my financial security. But, had one of those burritos slipped off my makeshift hotplate and rolled inside a jet engine, I

U.S. Air Force buddies (left to right)
Frank Cruz, Andy Gonzalez, and George Rosas

USAF buddies (left to right) Frank Cruz, Mitch Adler, and Andy Gonzales

would have had to declare my midnight snack attacks. I have no doubt my Air Force career would have ended abruptly and dishonorably.

In September of 1961, after three and a half years in the service, and a month before my 22nd birthday, I received my last orders. I was sent back to the States and stationed at Oxnard Air Force Base in California for my last six months in the military. Oxnard is just 60 miles north of East Los Angeles, a predominantly Mexican-American neighborhood. I could easily visit my Aunt Connie on the weekends. Since she and her husband Brad Moorehead owned a few used-car lots in the area, they could loan me a car, and I began to explore East Los Angeles. I soon knew I would not be returning to the dreaded heat of the Arizona desert.

The importance of those years was my development of a sense of country, an appreciation for the diversity of our nation, and an understanding of the world. No question, the military had a profound impact on me in that regard. I had easily adapted to the discipline and regimentation of the military that was not unlike my hardworking teenage years.

Also, it had become abundantly clear to me that more stripes on a uniform meant better quality jobs and that one way to earn those stripes was to take college courses. No one in Barrio Hollywood had attended college, but the military provided me with some new role models.

The idea began to emerge that an acceptable reason for not returning to Arizona would be to get settled with Aunt Connie and Uncle Brad Moorehead and use my GI Bill benefits at the nearby East Los Angeles College. The GI Bill, or the Servicemen's Readjustment Act of 1944, has been the great equalizer. For me and thousands of others, a free college education was our ticket to becoming a member of the middle class in the United States.

Not long after I joined the Air Force, Mom married Modesto "Tito" Peralta, who had been a regular customer at Columbia Café. Dicky was married by that time too and was working for the City of Tucson Parks and Recreation Department.

My mother's model of an organized and disciplined approach to life played out in just the right sequence to benefit the three of us. Her influence would again ensure me an easy transition, this time to an academic life.

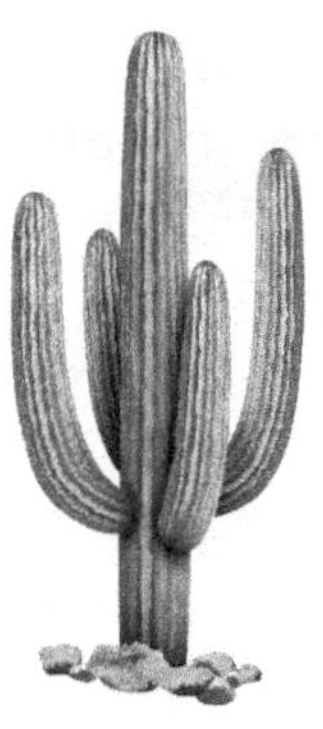

Chapter Three

My Life's Work Begins

It was no secret in my family that I had grown to love Southern California. After having spent so much time with Aunt Connie and Uncle Brad during the summers of my last years of high school and weekends during my Oxnard Air Force Base assignment, their East Los Angeles home was a comfortable place to begin my life after military service.

With the benefit of the GI Bill and California's basically free college tuition, in those days, I enrolled at East Los Angeles College (ELAC). I lived with Aunt Connie and Uncle Brad for the remainder of 1961 and all of 1962. The following year, I moved to my own apartment on West El Repetto Drive, which forms the northern border of the college campus, in the more affluent city of Monterey Park. My roommates were two fellow students who I met at the central gathering place on campus, the "Dog House." We were, after all, the East Los Angeles Huskies.

Not long after my classes began, a classmate introduced me to my future wife and life partner, Bonnie Baldwin. The gorgeous redhead, from the South Pasadena area, seemed out of my league. But some months later I gathered the courage to ask her out on a date. Neither of us can remember the name of the place, but our first date was a dinner at a Mexican restaurant on Atlantic Boulevard between Beverly and Whittier. We were both dedicated students, which may be why the relationship didn't get serious until late 1963. Bonnie and I married on April 24, 1964, while still ELAC students.

With my bride, Bonnie Baldwin, on evening of our wedding day

My initial academic plan to declare a pre-dental major had been encouraged by a dentist and mentor Dr. Lionel Ballesteros. The big idea started with a toothache. I complained about a sore tooth to my classmate Priscilla Barragán. I had not known she was a dental assistant at a local office. Priscilla urged me to make an appointment with her boss right away. My first visit to Ballesteros Dental went well, and the doctor and I struck up a friendship after discovering that we were both from Arizona. Dr. Ballesteros suggested that I consider becoming a dentist. The entrepreneurial spirit in me liked the sound of having my own practice.

Dr. Ballesteros and I met several times at his dental office, which was just a couple of blocks off campus on Atlantic Boulevard. He took the time to map out the classes I should take. I was very interested in the proposed coursework—zoology, biology, physics, and inorganic chemistry. But I was soon to meet my nemesis—organic chemistry.

I had enjoyed inorganic chemistry and creating synthetic products by introducing various catalysts. But organic chemistry, the basis of all earthly life, was going to be the death of me. Understanding "life" (materials that contain carbon atoms), and the chemical reactions to it, sounds important and fascinating, right? But the whole process of learning carbon's single, double, and triple bonding patterns just didn't interest me at all.

Certainly, today, I can appreciate the enormous range of commercial applications derived from the study of the structural and property reactions of organic compounds. But I was busy falling in love, and not just with Bonnie Baldwin. I had begun enrolling in some of the required social science courses and had met the professor who would help me identify my true vocation.

I hated to disappoint him, but Dr. Ballesteros could detect that I was losing interest in the path to becoming a dentist. Pricilla was taking a lot of the same courses, and I think she must have shared my frustration with her boss. I continued to visit him from time to time because he wanted me to come in and give him an update, which I was happy to do since after dropping organic chemistry my grades were excellent.

I always enjoyed meeting with Dr. Ballesteros. We often spoke about the precarious international political scene. I had been paying close attention to President Kennedy's warnings of the 1962 Cuban Missile Crisis, and I could offer the perspective of one who had guarded our fleet of F-104 jets in Asia.

In my third semester at ELAC I learned of President Kennedy's assassination. As I passed the Dog House on my way to an English class, it seemed like the whole campus was crying. My mind was spinning. American presidents aren't murdered, and yet it had happened on that November day in 1963.

Hours after hearing the terrible news, I saw footage of Jacqueline Kennedy in her iconic Chanel suit spattered with her husband's blood. I immediately remembered Mrs. Kennedy's ability and the opportunities she took to speak Spanish at public events, which had endeared the young couple to so many. In addition, many of my East Los Angeles College classmates and their families had experienced so much pride in having a Catholic president for the first time in the country. That didn't register with me so much at the time of his death, but I do remember during his presidential campaign that there were people who worried that Jack Kennedy would have divided loyalty between the pope in Vatican City and our government in Washington, D.C.

I had been more impressed with his proposals to help the poor in our country and in developing nations through his Peace Corps challenge, his initiatives to ensure more Americans attained higher education, and his inspiring rally to reach for the stars, literally. His assassination was truly stunning to me. I was never the same after his death. My awareness of social issues became a driving force in my life. My acceptance that life is short caused me to pursue, with vigor, opportunities to contribute.

By then I was taking some of Professor Helen Miller Bailey's history classes. She made the subject matter so interesting that it drove me and many classmates to learn ever more and more. "Doc" Bailey was a Latin American scholar, a rare breed among history professors at that time. Her lessons about Aztec and Mayan civilizations were nothing short of thrilling to her Mexican American students. As young adults, so many of us were the sons and daughters of those folks who had come north from México after the revolution of 1910 and started their families in the United States in the 1940s. Prior to sitting in Doc Bailey's classes, our collective history had been essentially absent from our formal and state-sponsored education.

Helen Miller Bailey "Doc" with one of several textbooks she authored

So, I was there at ELAC and taking my studies very seriously, frustrated with organic chemistry, leaning more towards the influence of historian Helen Miller Bailey, and being devastated by the murder of our young, idealistic president. I changed my major from pre-dental to history and never looked back. That was the moment that I began my life's work to illuminate the Latino experience.

I've always called East Los Angeles College "the Chicano Harvard of the West." That nickname is understandable when a short list of career achievements of Latino alumni is reviewed.

- United States Ambassador to México and Los Angeles Unified School District President Dr. Julian Nava
- Community activist and Los Angeles County Supervisor Gloria Molina
- President/CEO Mexican American Legal Defense Fund (MALDEF) and President/CEO of California Foundation Antonia Hernández
- Award-winning actor, director, and activist Edward James Olmos
- Los Angeles Mayor Antonio Villaraigosa
- ARCO Director of Governmental Affairs, President and Chief Executive Officer of the United States-México Chamber of Commerce Albert C. Zapanta, PhD.
- Orthopedic surgeon Richard Zapanta, M.D.
- California State Assembly and Senate Member, and California Democratic Party Chairman Arthur "Art" Torres
- United States Ambassador to UNESCO, Special Assistant to President Jimmy Carter, and United States Congressman Esteban Torres

- Writer and Poet Laureate of City of Los Angeles Luís Rodríguez
- President/CEO Cordoba Corporation George Pla

I made some great friends at ELAC, including the Zapanta brothers, Richard and Eddie, who lived on Brooklyn Avenue (later renamed César Chávez Boulevard), which formed the southern border of the college campus. They were both quite brilliant and bright stars from Garfield High School, one of the historically underserved eastside schools. Richard had declared a pre-med major at ELAC, and later graduated from USC Keck School of Medicine and opened his orthopedic surgery practice in Monterey Park, where he continues to serve patients in his home neighborhood.

The brothers introduced me to one of their cousins Al Zapanta, who like me, was interested in the social sciences. When it came time to transfer to a four-year university from ELAC, I could have gone to the University of California, Los Angeles (UCLA), but Al and I ended up enrolling together at the University of Southern California (USC), Professor Bailey's alma mater. Al later became a decorated Vietnam veteran and a successful business man.

Bonnie and I lived in the East Los Angeles area after we got married. Bonnie had earned her Associate of Arts degree and began applying for secretarial or executive assistant jobs. As a finalist for one position, she was interviewed by a senior executive of the Los Angeles Department of Water and Power (LADWP) in downtown Los Angeles. Unbeknownst to Bonnie, the executive was a graduate of USC. In the normal course of interview questions, at a time when marital status was not an off-limits query for young women, Bonnie relayed that she was a graduate of Franklin High School and ELAC, and that I was studying at USC. That apparently sealed the deal. Bonnie worked for the head of department for several years.

Soon after her hiring, we moved back to El Repetto, the northern border of the ELAC campus. We both had cars, but often she would take me to campus, circle back to LADWP headquarters and then pick me up at the end of her day during my undergrad work in 1964 and 1965.

Through the winters of 1966 and 1967, I earned my teaching credential. In the process, I had done some student teaching at Foshay Junior High School near USC, followed by a semester-long assignment at Westchester High School, on the more affluent west side of Los Angeles. I had the good fortune to have been mentored by a master teacher Dolores Tucker.

Now with a teaching credential in 1967, my own job search began. Recruiters from different school districts visited the USC campus on Career Day. I was able to set up a meeting with Los Angeles Unified School District Recruiter Neil Schambaugh. "Oh, Mr. Cruz, you've done very well and at the top of your class," he said after reviewing my résumé. He asked a lot of questions about my student teaching experiences and ultimately, we got down to available job opportunities. Mr. Schambaugh explained that there were not a lot of openings, but with my academic record he was sure he could secure a spot for me at one of the westside schools. Since he knew I had worked at Westchester High, he knew that I understood that that meant modern facilities, a more homogenous student population, lower dropout rates, and just an overall kinder and gentler experience than the underserved schools in the downtown and eastside campuses of Los Angeles.

He was visibly shocked when I replied, "That's nice Mr. Schambaugh, but I want to teach at either Garfield, Lincoln, or Roosevelt high schools." My idea was that as a man who looked like the eastside students' fathers and uncles, this was where I belonged and where I could make a difference. I had to repeat myself a few times before it was clear that I was quite serious. That fall of 1967, I started my teaching career at Lincoln High School in East Los Angeles. That was a good thing because we had recently moved near the Alhambra/ South Pasadena border. The short commute to Lincoln was helpful since our first child, Heather, had just been born.

In the spring of 1968, I was teaching at Lincoln High School when student frustration with neglected eastside campuses, and the lack of any history of Latin Americans, indeed, Latin Americans were completely absent from school curriculum, resulted in the infamous East Los Angeles Walkouts of 1968. The late sixties were a time of intense cultural awareness throughout the country. Television news broadcast the civil rights marches and other non-violent protests of African Americans, which were often met with violent policing. Hispanics were beginning to question why the schools in their neighborhoods were under-served when compared to those on the affluent westside of Los Angeles. Americans, young and old, were protesting the Vietnam War and the tragic assassinations of Medgar Evers, President Kennedy, Malcolm X, and Che Guevara.

That was the social climate in which I was teaching history to both eighth and eleventh graders. The older students' textbook, by Henry Commager Steele, included a chapter on immigration and how it shaped our nation. I struggled. Looking out at those faces of Garcías, Rodríguezes, Hernándezes, and Maldonados I only had lecture material about Western European immigration to the Southwestern United States. The problem was not that their book was wrong, it was just woefully incomplete. There I was in this classroom of kids with nothing published to share with them about how their families had come to live in the Southwest, in many cases, hundreds of years before European settlers.

This dilemma was the impetus for a second critical decision in my teaching career. I was presented with the opportunity to shed light on Mexican heritage and immigration, but I needed to make it happen myself. Clearly, the school district had chosen that textbook, and as a new teacher I was savvy enough to know that they would not be making a change based on Frank Cruz's complaints.

A search for a more complete academic work to augment my eleventh-graders' history lessons inevitably lead to Professor Helen Miller Bailey's seminal text, *Latin American Civilization,* which she co-authored in 1955 with Abraham P. Nasatir. The history was all there but written at the university level. I could find no other text. I decided to visit my old history professor and Latin American scholar at East Los Angeles College Professor Bailey, who coincidentally had earned her doctorate and master teacher credential at USC some 30 years earlier. I thought "Doc," as we all called her, might know of some supplemental reading materials.

She quickly scheduled a meeting with me, and I remember complaining that my required textbook was incomplete. With that twinkle in her eye, well-known to her many admiring students, Doc replied, "Well, then, I guess we'll just have to write one." And that's what happened. Her publisher, Houghton Mifflin, coordinated narrowing her college-level text for the high school level.

I began researching and writing the chapters on the post-colonial period and immigration to the United States, based on the economic push and pull of the fluctuating need for labor in the Southwest. I would handwrite the chapters and Bonnie would type them up. I would use the mimeograph machine at school to make enough copies for the class. Then I would explain to my students, "Okay for tomorrow's class, you'll need to read Chapter 8 in your textbook and these two pages I'm handing out now. These pages detail factors relevant to Latin Americans during the same time period."

Our book, *Latin Americans: Past and Present,* wasn't published until 1972. But the need for it, and subsequent research, inspired me to complete my masters' degree at USC, which I did in 1969. I immediately began to plan for a full-time teaching job and a part-time doctoral program.

Bailey and Cruz author *Latin Americans: past and present*

I began applying at California State Colleges. To be more precise, I applied for a faculty spot at Sonoma State University. I had been accepted into a doctorate program at both Stanford University and University of California, Berkeley, and it seemed possible to teach at nearby Sonoma State during the day and attend evening classes for a doctorate in history.

Before I left Lincoln High School, and during my last semester, Sal Castro, Anita Cano, Alicia López, and I organized a *ballet folklórico* class. We arranged performances that summer of 1969 at Sonoma State, where by then I had accepted a teaching position.

Along California Interstate 5 from Southern California up through the state's Central Valley, our bus of dancers encountered a farmworkers' protest march organized by César Chavez' United Farm Workers of America (UFW). Seizing a teachable moment, I made the bus driver pull over to the side of the road so that the students could see up close and personal labor rights activists.

Well-known Chicano photographer George Rodríquez was documenting the protest and snapped a picture of the bus with a student holding a sign out of the window. It read "HUELGA" or "STRIKE," in English. I never found out where the student got that sign. If you look very closely at the photo, you can see the back of my head in one of the windows. Because the photo had gotten around campus, I had some explaining to do when we returned to Lincoln High School

Lincoln High School folklórico students support UFW protestors

because the trip had been approved as a promotion of the arts and not a lesson in civil disobedience.

Remember, the 1968 East Los Angeles Walkouts had happened just one year before. Thousands of students, first from Wilson, then Lincoln, followed by Belmont, Garfield, and Roosevelt high schools simply walked off campus. They protested alongside many parents and siblings, for five days, and in the end delivered 13 demands to the Los Angeles Unified School Board. For serving as a mentor to the student organizers, social studies teacher at Lincoln High School Sal Castro was fired and banned from the district. Later he was justly re-instated.

Any activity that could be perceived as fomenting student unrest was highly frowned upon. Regardless of whether Lincoln's administrators believed my account of a roadside stop during that ballet folklórico fieldtrip, their rebuff was essentially mute because they would soon learn I was in the process of leaving Los Angeles for a professorship at Sonoma State.

That summer of 1969, little Heather was just 2 years old, and we moved up to the Bay Area for my new job. I was there at Sonoma State when I received a call from Sal Castro, my friend and former colleague at Lincoln. He told me that the Los Angeles affiliate of the NBC television network, KNBC-TV, had approached him to organize some professors of Chicano Studies to be filmed for an on-air lecture series as part of the station's *Sunrise Semester* programming that aired just before the *Today Show*. NBC and all the networks were required to fulfill what were called "public-interest obligations." The government required television stations to air some type of coverage or programs that were relevant to local audiences.

KNBC-TV Community Affairs Director Jay Rodríguez came up with the idea of filming a Chicano heritage series.

He asked Sal Castro if he would be a part of it. In the early seventies, as a part of that first wave of Chicano Studies professors, I felt the burden of what seemed like an unparalleled opportunity to make a difference in the lives of our students and our disenfranchised community. On an individual level, current events served to reinforce my commitment—to teach what and where I was most needed.

Sal did complain to me that he was unhappy with the low budget allocated to the production, and he did eventually step away from the project, but not before he had assembled several professors with specialized knowledge relevant to the Chicano community.

Professor Julian Nava, who had served as president of Los Angeles Unified School Board (even then the largest in the country), was assigned to the episode on education. Juan Gómez Quiñones covered Latino labor in America, Armando Morales focused on Latino justice, Tomas Martinez examined stereotyping of Chicanos in the media, and we went right down the line. Since my post-graduate research had been aimed at the study of the Mexican War (1846 to 1848) and immigration issues, I was assigned the episodes on those topics. Professor Fred Sánchez was very knowledgeable about the post-World War II years, so he was assigned the episode about zoot suit culture. In the end, ten of us were brought together at KNBC's offices.

During the first production meeting the question arose—do anyone of you want to be the host? I don't exactly remember how it was determined, but someone said something like, "Frank is a good talker," and I was designated as the host. In a brief meeting, on each day of filming, the lecturers would let me know the overall topics they were going to cover. We would then go into a studio that had been booked for two or three hours and we'd shoot two or three episodes. The executive producer was Cecilia Alvear. The producer was Ramón Ponce and production assistants were Alicia Sandoval, Rosa Sánchez, and Sue Estrada.

Each week the audience would see me welcoming the lecturer. It would go something like this: "Today we're going to cover education issues facing the Chicano community, and I have the pleasure of introducing Cal State University at Northridge history professor and Los Angeles Unified School Board Member Professor Julian Nava." When the lecture was completed, I would thank the professor and announce the topic and speaker that would air the following week.

Here was an opportunity to enlighten the public to the Latino experience and to explain what a Chicano was. I figured, if I'm doing it in the classroom and reaching a few hundred students a semester, on television I could inform literally thousands. The other professors felt similarly; we knew that this was a unique opportunity. In the beginning, the plan was for a ten-part series, but it soon blossomed into a 20-part series titled *Chicano I and II.*

Bound episodes of Chicano I & II series a gift from KNBC-TV

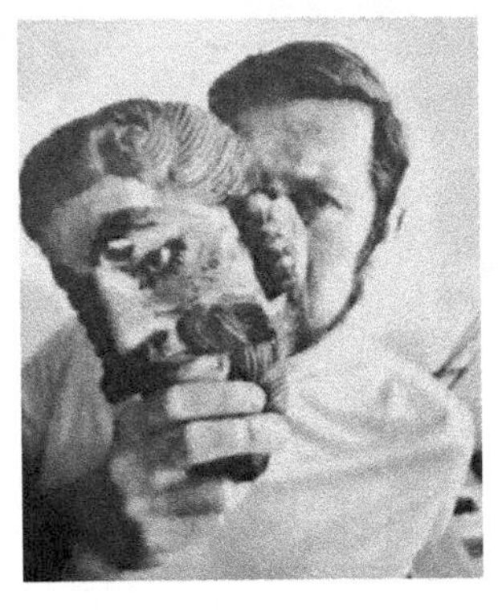

Chicano: Mexican Heritage*—Premiering July 10, at 5:00 P.M. KNBC presents a ten-part weekly series on the history of the Mexican-American or Chicano in the United States. The series looks at some of the contributions of the early Mexican settlers and what effect this had on American culture. The series will attempt to bridge the gap of misunderstanding, misconception, prejudice, discrimination, racism, fear, and distrust. In addition to looking at history from the Chicano standpoint, the series will also examine contemporary issues facing the Mexican-American community. Series host is Frank Cruz, associate professor of the Chicano Studies Department at Cal State Long Beach.*

Aztlan*—Host Frank Cruz introduces Jose H. Cuellar, M.A., Anthropology, University of California at Los Angeles, who describes the contributions made by Mexican ancestors in "Aztlan" or as we know it, the Western Hemisphere. The program also looks at the cultural influences made and how these influences have affected United States Southwest even in contemporary times.*

Myths of the Southwest*—Dispels the many popular myths about the Northwest México Territory (Southwest United States) that have been handed down unquestioned for several generations by American historians. Guest narrator is Richard Romo, San Fernando Valley State College, who explains that one of the myths has been one that glorifies the Anglo's contributions* *to American society, yet minimizes contributions made by other ethnic groups.*

Mexican American War Period—*Host Frank Cruz examines the Mexican American War of 1836. Myths, legends and half-truths associated with this period are examined. The reasons for the war, motives, fault, and what the war means to the Mexican resident of the United States today are also explored.*

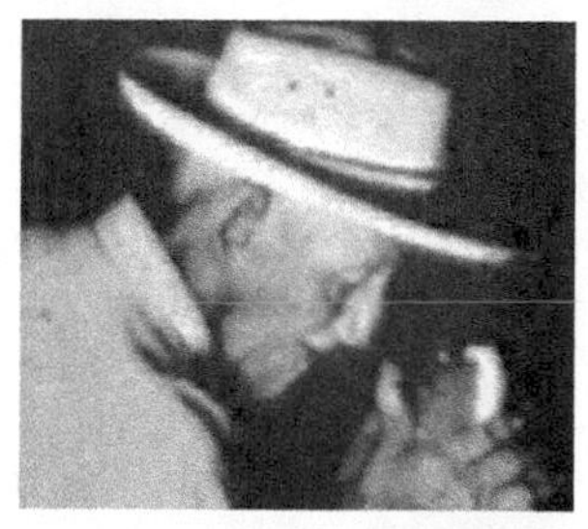

Conflict and Resistance: Myth of Docility—*This program deals with the period from 1848 to 1920 and documents the conflict between the Mexicano and the Anglo-American, highlighting the Mexican struggle for determination. Guest narrator is Carlos Arce, assistant professor and chairman, Chicano Studies Department, San Fernando Valley State College.*

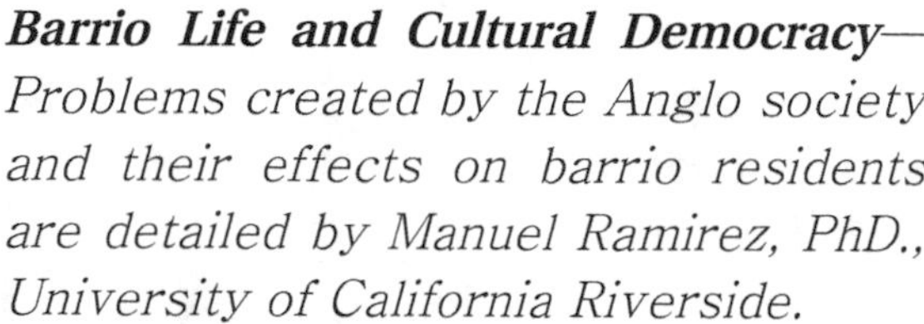

Barrio Life and Cultural Democracy—*Problems created by the Anglo society and their effects on barrio residents are detailed by Manuel Ramirez, PhD., University of California Riverside.*

Stereotyping in the Mass Media—*Dr. Tomas Martinez, assistant professor of sociology at Stanford University, examines the unfair way Chicanos have been portrayed in newspapers, movies, magazines and television.*

Spiders in the House—*The first program with a contemporary theme. It deals with the labor-manpower provided by the Mexicano in the economic and agricultural development of the area. The program looks specifically at history of the farm laborer, the migrant worker, and the reasons one had to take up this type of work. Guest is the noted historian and labor authority Dr. Ernesto Galarza.*

The War Years—*Guest is Frederico Sanchez, assistant professor of Chicano Studies at Cal State Long Beach. Sanchez traces the years during World War II, focusing on the era of the Mexican-American zoot suiter (also known as the "pachuco,") and contributions made to the war effort.*

Economic Repression of the Chicano—*Paul Sanchez, Dean, Graduate School of Social Work at San Jose State College, examines reasons for the low economic situation prevalent with most Chicanos and the braceros' effect on the farm labor market; education; employment discrimination by Anglo employers and unions; and what the future holds for the Chicano.*

Mexican-Americans and Education: Quo Vadis America?—*Experts discuss the failure of public education in the Mexican-American community. Guests are Ron Lopez, Director Mexican-American Center, Claremont Colleges; Dr. Simon Gonzalez, a UCLA Administrator; and Dr. Julian Nava, President, Board of Education of Los Angeles.*

What prompted NBC to do this 20-part series, aside from its public-service obligation, was that all institutions in society were under a lot of pressure to respond to the social responsibility that the American people, especially the youth, were demanding during those tumultuous years. The ten of us received no pay for our efforts, and ratings were apparently not a problem, so we weren't too surprised when KNBC executives chose to film the second set of ten lectures. I suppose it was just a project that KNBC could list to justify their license renewal in terms of programming. (In addition, the station could have used it to demonstrate some amount of diversity among their employees to respond to newly imposed reporting requirements of the Equal Employment Opportunity Commission, the agency established by the Civil Rights Act of 1964 to enforce the new federal law.)

Not only were both *Chicano I & II* the first productions of their kind by a national, commercial television station, but the series was aired in other major U.S. markets. I had thought the series was only going to be aired in Los Angeles, but other NBC stations in cities like Chicago, New York, and Miami picked it up as well.

Eight years later, the ABC television network broadcast the series, *Roots*. I can't help but compare and contrast *Chicano I & II* with Alex Haley's epic television series. The ABC network spent more than $6 million on that production in 1977; whereas, KNBC-TV spent just a few hundred dollars on our educational series in 1969. Both series dealt with minority subject matter and both have been slighted in some ways. Controversy has surrounded author Alex Haley's non-fictional claim of certain details of his family's slavery experience in America. And the epic *Chicano I & II* are never mentioned as "breakthrough" television programming, which the series clearly was.

Similar parallels can be drawn from the legal environment relative to education. In 1947, a Federal Appeals Court in California held that the forced segregation of students into separate "Mexican schools" was unconstitutional and unlawful. The Méndez family had brought suit against the Westminster School District, in Orange County, because their light-skinned children were enrolled in the "white" school, but their three younger children with darker complexions were rejected and forced to attend the "Mexican" school that was run down and offered classes consistent with the idea that these students could only aspire to low-paid service jobs. The white school, by contrast, offered courses that would prepare students for college acceptance.

In Méndez v Westminster, Appellate Court Judge Paul J. McCormick ruled: "The equal protection of the laws pertaining to the public-school system in California is not provided by furnishing in separate schools the same technical facilities, textbooks and courses of instruction to children of Mexican ancestry that are available to the other public-school children regardless of their ancestry. A paramount requisite in the American system of public education is social equality. It must be open to all children by unified school association regardless of lineage."

My point in bringing up the Méndez case is that very few Americans have heard of the momentous ruling. But most people are aware of the "groundbreaking" 1954 Supreme Court case Brown v Board of Education that declared that "separate but equal" schools were not providing all students an equal education and were indeed unconstitutional. To truly understand the irony of these cases, the history of Mexican immigration to the United States must be examined with some vigor.

But to summarize here, we know that once it was clear that the United States was going to enter World War II, the government recognized the need for workers to maintain farms and work in U.S. factories while hundreds of thousands of young men were serving in Europe, Africa, and Asia. Therefore, for the purpose of immigration policies, the Roosevelt administration lobbied hard to continue the classification of Mexicans as part of the "white" race. In doing so, Mexicans could by-pass the immigration restrictions on non-whites, which had been in place since World War I (when the same need for labor had existed).

So, you could say that the court's decision in Méndez v Westminster outlawed the discriminatory practice of designating schools for those "white" students who were of brown heritage. And Brown v Board of Education outlawed designating separate schools for all people of color. Indeed, I once asked former Supreme Court Justice Sandra Day O'Connor about the Méndez v Westminster case.

Justice O'Connor and I spent several hours together at a conference where we had both been asked to speak. We got into quite a conversation after we realized that we were both raised in Tucson, Arizona. Justice O'Connor grew up on a ranch outside of town with several Mexican American employees. I was surprised to learn that by the time she entered elementary school, she was fluent in both English and Spanish. In response to my question, she made it quite clear that the Méndez case had laid the legal foundation for Brown v Board of Education.

With Supreme Court Justice Sandra Day O'Connor at a Fred Friendly Seminars conference

While touching on the topic of the war years, I should point out that in 1969, *Chicano I & II* covered the World War II years and America's highly decorated Latino soldiers. Yet their bravery was not addressed in the media again until my Emmy-award winning series on NBC-TV titled *The Latinization of Los Angeles*. My five-part series included a segment that highlighted that more than any other ethnic group, on a percentage basis, Mexican Americans earned the nation's highest honor—the Medal of Honor. The topic wasn't addressed again until the fall of 2013 when an episode of the six-hour PBS series, *Latino Americans* highlighted the Latino experience in the military. But I jump ahead.

In 1969 to 1970, I was teaching at Sonoma State under the presumption that I would soon begin a doctoral program at Stanford or the Berkeley. Although each university had accepted me, both had assumed that I intended to be a full-time, daytime student. My responsibilities as a husband and father made that impossible. Rather than give up on my goal of a doctoral degree, I had to tell Bonnie and little Heather that we were going back to Southern California. I was sure I could teach and resume part-time work on my doctoral program in the evenings at USC. Not long after we re-established ourselves in an apartment in South Pasadena, I received a call from the dean at California State University, Long Beach, with an offer to fill the new position of Chicano Studies department chair. I gladly accepted.

In fact, many of the professors who had participated in *Chicano I & II* were tapped for these, what I call, battlefield assignments in the California State College system. I would be remiss if I did not point out that there were no women among those first Chicano Studies departments.

Our subject matter was not yet viewed, at least in those early years, as a legitimate field of study. The University of California at Los Angeles would have been perhaps a more logical campus for such programs to be developed in Southern California, but the University of California system and its Board of Regents were simply not as nimble and couldn't be as responsive to the demands of a changing society as could the California State Colleges.

We were basically plucked out of our new professor positions and made "department heads" with all the academic prestige that comes with such titles. Yet we were working alongside other professors who had waited years to be so sanctified or had simply been summarily passed over. These appointments caused a lot of resentment against us, and we received very little assistance as we added to our duties as teachers the roles as administrators. We also experienced a good deal of push back from the traditional history faculty whose work was being questioned as being incomplete.

So as courageous soldiers in battle, we depended on each other for our success. A few had come before us with important groundwork that we could build on to form our programs. In 1967, anthropologist Octavio Romano and Nick Vaca began publishing a Chicano studies journal called *El Grito: A Journal of Contemporary Mexican-American Thought.* Also, in 1967, political science professor Ralph Guzmán was teaching at California State College at Los Angeles and working on the Mexican American study at UCLA, funded by the Ford Foundation, and completing a doctoral thesis, which would become the foundation for a national center for Chicano Studies at the university.

In the fall of 1969, many of us attended a conference at the University of California, Santa Bárbara campus, as a follow-up to an earlier conference that spring. In response to student, community, and faculty demands, the conference attendees produced "El Plan de Santa Bárbara," which served as a guideline for Chicano Studies curriculum. We agreed to correct the pattern of historical neglect and reject erroneous social science research since the existing data had been collected only from rural inhabitants, whereas millions of Latinos resided in urban centers.

It was an exciting time to be a Mexican American in California for those Chicano authors and professors in Chicano Studies degree programs. At California State University at Northridge there was Rudy Acuña, Raul Ruiz, Jorge García, and Julian Nava. California State University Long Beach began its programs with Frank Sandoval, Fred Sánchez, Joe López, Al Osuna, and me. Other universities in Northern California's

Bay Area and in Los Angeles offered a few Chicano Studies courses and some like UCLA, USC, Stanford, and Berkeley created Chicano Studies centers or programs. And in 1970, UCLA began publishing an influential journal titled *Aztlan: A Journal of Chicano Studies*. These works and many others formed the basis for the first academic degree programs initially offered only at California State Colleges at Northridge and Long Beach.

My world view had expanded exponentially when I left Barrio Hollywood for the U.S. Airforce and later as an educator in California. I began to witness that struggling with or against assimilation into white American culture was a big hurdle and the cause of much angst among my students and many Latino leaders I knew. So many times, while teaching the "complete" history of California at Lincoln High School in East Los Angeles and in the California State College system, students had visited my office in obvious distress. More than one student told me,

> "Mr. Cruz, I don't know who I am, or who I even want to be. I live one life at home while on the streets and here on campus it's like an alternative universe. Most of my school friends don't know that my parents don't speak English. They talk about their parents who are professionals, but I have never even met a lawyer or an engineer."

Awakening these first-generation college students to their Mexican heritage with lectures about the magnificent and ancient Mayan and Aztec civilizations only exacerbated their confusion.

> "Why am I not proud of my parents?" they asked me. "Why don't I know anything about the towns they came from in México? After 12 years of schooling,

why am I just learning about the real history of México and California?"

While I felt honored that so many students were comfortable confiding their deep torment, my heart broke with each question, each so fundamental to their very existence. They wanted to know who they were.

To understand their bewilderment, it's important to consider the political and societal context relative to Mexican Americans preceding and culminating in the tumultuous 1960s. Mexican Americans were omitted from mainstream politics in California, with less than 20 Hispanics having served in the California legislature between 1849 and 1963. According to Alex Vassar at the California State Library, 13 of those 20 were no longer in office by the start of America's Civil War. In fact, there was not a single Latino in the California state legislature between 1912 and 1963. In 1950, the lone Chicano on the Los Angeles City Council was Edward Roybal. He was the first Mexican American elected to the council since 1881 and he would be the last for another 20 years.

In the broader view, the national civil rights discussion had been centered strictly on the chasm between blacks and whites. Indeed, Mexican Americans weren't declared a minority and were rather lumped together with all "others." What precious little literature about our population that existed focused on rural life, ignoring the fact that most Chicanos were living in cities. The 1965 UCLA *Mexican American Study Project* reported the absence of not only data on Mexican Americans but on the absence of Mexican American social scientists. Co-director of the project, Joan W. Moore, explained, "Our colleague, Ralph Guzmán, was to become the very first Chicano political scientist, and there weren't many more Mexican American sociologists or economists."

So that handful of us in the late 1960s who were accepting battlefield assignments as Chicano Studies professorships at California colleges were emerging out of a total absence of academic focus, except that which we had developed ourselves. We certainly had examples of social scientists and historians at black colleges, and there were a few of us who were achieving a college education because of the GI Bill. But essentially, we were building programs where none had existed about a population from which very little data had been gathered.

Thus, the floodgates were opened to irrigate a vast field of study. And as those students and young people who had a burning desire to know who they were came pouring in to our classroom; the ground beneath their feet was about to turn muddy and unstable.

Students and professors, alike, were deeply affected by the events of the 1960s. Americans were devastated by the assassination of President John F. Kennedy. The large percentage of Mexican Americans who were Catholic experienced perhaps a special kind of hopelessness when the first Catholic to live in the White House was murdered in 1963. Five years later, we suffered an inconceivable blow when Kennedy's younger brother, Bobby, who had been greeted by thousands in East Los Angeles just hours before he, too, was gunned down just after being pronounced the winner of the California Democratic Party presidential primary election.

In a mass protest in 1968, thousands of high school students walked out of their classrooms to protest curriculum and textbooks that excluded their heritage. They also called for the end to discriminatory treatment in the classroom and protested the unequal resources afforded schools on the eastside of Los Angeles, when compared to the schools in the more affluent western portion of Los Angeles Unified School District.

At the same time, it did not go unnoticed by the community that Chicano soldiers were dying in Vietnam at a much higher rate than other ethnic groups. Jungle warfare scenes, along with the endless body bags being loaded onto aircraft, filled the evening television news. Opposition to the war sparked the first mass protest by Latinos in the United States.

The Chicano Moratorium Committee and other Chicano anti-war activist groups and individuals, like Ralph Guzmán in 1969, sought media focus on studies that revealed the numbers of Mexican Americans who were drafted and who were dying at disproportionate rates; reportedly 20 percent of Vietnam War casualties were Mexican Americans who at the time made up just 10 percent of the population.

On August 29, 1970, some 30,000 activists, students, and many families with young children marched south in peaceful protest along Atlantic Boulevard and then turned west on famed Whittier Boulevard in East Los Angeles. The march ended with speeches and entertainment in Laguna Park, which was soon to be renamed Rubén Salazar Park.

Sadly, though the march had been approved by the authorities, the local police and Los Angeles County sheriffs, reacted badly. Six people were killed, including Rubén Salazar who was a beloved journalist for his groundbreaking reporting on the Mexican American community. He had served as a voice for the broad coalition of Mexican-American groups in opposition to the Vietnam War—Chicano Moratorium—at the *Los Angeles Times* newspaper and in his role as news director at Los Angeles' Spanish-language television station KMEX-TV. As Salazar and his television news crew rested at the end of the day in a nearby café, police, reportedly without warning, launched tear gas projectiles into the café. The coroner's inquest later revealed that one of the nine and a half inch long, inch and a half diameter tear gas "bombs" tore completely through Rubén Salazar's head causing massive brain damage and death.

The first community account and a graphic depiction of the violence on August 29, 1970, *Requiem 29*, was a documentary produced by Móctezuma Esparza and directed by my cousin David García. David was a teacher in Chapman University's film school and had also worked in the production department at KNBC-TV. David's father was the son of one of my dad's sisters. *Requiem 29* was a well-publicized documentary that remained very popular for many years. The biopic was compiled from a variety of sources and included video clips from filmmaker Jesús Treviño's footage of the Salazar murder inquest, which he filmed as part of his television news coverage for public broadcasting station KCET Los Angeles. Treviño, soon after, produced an hour-long PBS special that summarized the Salazar inquest, *Chicano Moratorium: The Aftermath.*

At the time, I had no idea that in just a couple of years I would follow in Rubén Salazar footsteps by reporting on the Chicano experience on television, rather than in print.

National news provided no calming effect on my students. Civil rights marches were taking place across the country and often elicited military-like responses from federal and local law enforcement. The assassinations of Malcolm X by Nation of Islam followers in 1965; Che Guevara by Bolivian military guided by the CIA in 1967; and Reverend Martin Luther King Jr. by James Earl Ray in 1968 were followed by the murder of four protesting Kent State students by National Guard troops in 1970.

In 1971, the *New York Times* published the "Pentagon Papers," which revealed a troubling account of our, by then, decades-old involvement in Vietnam (going back to President Truman) just at a time when great numbers of the population were questioning the legal and moral justification for intensifying U.S. intervention in Southeast Asia. Virtually at the same time, the *Washington Post* was revealing daily what turned out to be a burglary, sanctioned at the highest levels, of the headquarters of the Democratic National Committee's offices in the Watergate Hotel in Washington, D.C. The protracted investigation and massive cover-up undertaken by the administration, ultimately brought down the Richard Nixon presidency.

To say it was a tumultuous time is hardly adequate to describe the reality of the mid-to-late sixties.

And yet, I can't say that I ever experienced seeking the kind of defining moment that some of my students were pursuing. I never had doubts about who I was. I think that was largely because I had not grown up in a metropolitan area with the exposure to different cultures, such as my Los Angeles-born students were trying to navigate. I am the son of Mexican immigrants who came to the United States after the Mexican Revolution of 1910. My identity was very clear early on. In my case, living in that cocoon of Barrio Hollywood, I had basically thought everyone was Mexican.

Unlike most of my students, Spanish was my first language and the only language I heard anywhere growing up on the west side of Tucson, except in our classrooms. I was wrapped tightly in a Mexican blanket. That never-wavering concept of who I was, combined with the model of hard work paying off for my mom, grounded me in self-respect and self-efficacy that has been the foundation from which I experienced the sixties and since have explored the worlds of education, journalism, and business.

Part II

Chapter Four

But I Don't Know Anything About Journalism

One afternoon during the 1971 fall semester at California State University, Long Beach, I returned from lunch off campus and my assistant handed me a phone message. The news director at KABC-TV had called me a few minutes before. I was chair of the Chicano Studies department, teaching a few history courses, and working on my doctorate at the University of Southern California (USC). My first reaction to the message was that there might be a student demonstration happening on campus.

In the 1970s, student demonstrations were common occurrences on college campuses all around the country. Sit-ins at the offices of college presidents, with students demanding more academic freedom, highlighting civil rights concerns, and protests against the Vietnam War were all possibilities. So, rather than appear uncooperative with the press, I hurried into my office and returned the call to Bill Fyfe at KABC-TV.

I would later come to appreciate Bill Fyfe's direct communications style but, in this initial phone conversation, I was a bit startled by how quickly he got to the point.

"Are you the Mr. Cruz who hosted the Chicano heritage television series on NBC?" he asked. Consistent with this direct approach, Bill had created the *Eyewitness News* format mirrored by television stations around the country. He had condensed the 4-minute segments into, the now standard, 1.5-minute slots with reporters at the scene and on camera. In that call Bill did explain that he had seen a rerun of that Chicano series.

"Yes, that's me," I replied.

Without a pause, Bill asked, "Mr. Cruz, would you be interested in a career in journalism?" I replied, "Sir, I am a historian and a professor; I don't know anything about journalism." He didn't seem to think that was a problem.

"We can teach you all that," he said. "Mr. Cruz, the television industry is changing. Here at KABC we're bringing in lawyers to present consumer reports and meteorologists, like Dr. George Fischbeck, to do the weather. And we'd like to hire someone like you with the academic background and the Spanish language to cover stories relevant to the Hispanic community we're trying to attract."

I repeated that I didn't know anything about television reporting and he said, "Well, won't you just come up to the station and discuss what I'm proposing." Because of my usual willingness to be open-minded and my pride in the work we had done on that Chicano history series, I agreed to meet at KABC-TV's station in Los Angeles.

Bill's office was enclosed but located in the very center

of the large newsroom. To say it was an energetic environment is an understatement. Writers, editors, and videographers were engaged in a variety of activities preparing news for the on-air reporters. In fact, I recognized several there in the newsroom from watching them on television. This seemed to me a very exciting collaborative environment, particularly when compared to the mostly solitary daily life in my office at the university. I became increasingly interested in what Mr. Fyfe had to say.

"You know the subject matter and you know the community," he explained. "You're just who we're looking for to focus on the issues of the Hispanic community in and around Los Angeles." He was trying to win me over and the conversation began to develop a chorus of me repeating that I knew nothing about journalism, followed by a verse to assure me that, "we can teach you those skills." Finally, I asked if he would give me some time to think it over, and he agreed.

As I rose to shake his hand and exit the office, Bill reached in his jacket breast pocket and pulled out a slip of paper and handed it to me. "Perhaps this will help you make your decision. This is the AFTRA annual salary schedule for each of the three-year contracts we are offering you." The American Federation of Television and Radio Artists, or AFTRA, later merged with the Screen Actors Guild, or SAG, in 2015.

I looked at the numbers and tried to conceal my reaction.

Decisions, Decisions

Man, did I have a lot to think about.

"Supportive" doesn't really explain my wife Bonnie's role in my career moves or the intensity of the 12 months preceding that call from Bill Fyfe. I had just earned my master's degree at USC in May 1970 and was accepted as a Ph.D.

candidate. I had a committee of esteemed professors, a plan, and the whole shot at an academic career. However, a buddy of mine Ernie Martínez and I had set our sights on getting our doctoral degrees at Berkeley or Stanford because both universities had renowned history programs. To try to make that happen, I had applied for a teaching position at Sonoma State in Northern California and at California State Long Beach, in Southern California, as a back-up. I was offered both positions in 1969.

The conversation at USC was difficult because so much planning and faculty time had already been devoted to developing my Ph.D. program there. But I had my heart set on Berkeley or Stanford for my doctoral work. In the end, we packed up our house and Heather, who was three years old at the time, and left our home in South Pasadena for Northern California.

The plan had been that I would teach full time at Sonoma State and begin a Ph.D. program at Berkeley or Stanford on a part-time basis. Well, basically as soon as we got settled, I found out that neither school was amenable to my part-time limitation. It was just an absolute "no" from both. Not working would have been impossible because Bonnie was pregnant with twins. We were soon to be a family of five. I contacted the dean at Cal State Long Beach who was willing to take me on, and we headed back down to South Pasadena in the fall of 1971. USC accepted me back into the Ph.D. program and we started looking for a house nearer to the Long Beach campus.

Our twins, Frankie and Vanessa, were born on June 26, 1971, and we moved into a new house in Fountain Valley over the July 4th weekend. This was not on an executive relocation package—this was Bonnie, me, a couple of friends, and a U-Haul rented truck, and twin babies less than one week old.

Gosh, the electricity hadn't even been turned on the first day. We actually had to ask our new next-door neighbors, Dorothy and Ed Nix, if we could borrow their stove to warm formula for the twins!

I chaired the Long Beach State Chicano Studies department, taught classes on Mondays and Wednesdays, and attended my own classes on Tuesdays and Thursdays at USC. Needless to say, I was fully engaged in academics, which left Bonnie with her hands full on the home front.

During all this time I had regular contact with the college professor who was the reason I had become a history teacher in the first place. I was writing a textbook with Latin American scholar Professor Helen Miller Bailey to tell, for the first time, the full history of the American Southwest, including the influence of Spain and ultimately the Mexican people. I had a calling, if you will, to ensure that my students and their families learned about the glorious, albeit often tragic, story of their ancestry and its impact on what became California, Arizona, and Texas.

So, as I considered Bill Fyfe's offer, I reasoned that I was teaching about 120 students in my three or four classes per semester; whereas, KABC-TV was offering me a chance to do the same thing but for literally thousands.

The KABC-TV offer also intrigued my entrepreneurial spirit, inherited from my mother, as well as my own internal drive to excel, which for me meant never accepting second-class citizenship as a Chicano. If Bill Fyfe was true to his word, I could become the first Latino television on-air reporter to exclusively cover the Hispanic community in the United States.

I discussed the KABC-TV offer with my dean at Cal State Long Beach. Bonnie and I were comforted by the university being open to granting me a leave of absence that meant I could return to teaching if television reporting didn't work out.

I must admit that the first-year AFTRA salary, which was nearly three times what I was making at the college, also influenced my decision.

Facing my doctoral board at USC however, was uncomfortable at best. Good people had stuck their necks out for me a second time, and I now had to explain, again, why I was not going through with the program.

I called KABC-TV News Director Bill Fyfe and accepted the reporter position.

Little did I realize I was jumping from the proverbial frying pan into the fire, or what I like to call another "battlefield assignment." I had thought that being anointed chair of a department that had not previously existed and without having sort of paid my dues so to speak at that university put me in an untenable position vis-à-vis my peers. Certainly, that was the case. But, television journalism, much like the entertainment industry, is quite an incestuous system. In those days, you basically needed to be related to someone in the union you hoped to join in order to secure entry.

I had thought that because the station manager and network executives in New York wanted me and my interest in the Latino community, that my new colleagues would welcome my brown face to their white clan. I guess unconsciously I had the expectation that surely the workplace, regardless of the industry, outside of the confines of academia, would foster the egalitarian culture I had experienced in the Air Force. With a few exceptions, nothing could have been further from the truth.

Shining a Light

Up to that point in late 1970, Los Angeles media outlets could claim only a handful of Hispanics among their ranks. Bob Navarro at CBS station KNXT-TV was a familiar face in Los Angeles. Joe Ramírez manned the assignment desk at KNBC-TV and was promoted to a field reporter in 1969. Joel García was a reporter for KNBC-TV in 1968 and then moved on to KTTV. In June 1970 Henry Alfaro began his journalist career at KABC-TV.

On radio we enjoyed sisters Inez Pedroza at KRLA and Cecilia Pedroza on KFWB. Then there was Frank del Olmo who had started his journalism studies at UCLA, but later when the university terminated its journalism program, he transferred to San Fernando Valley State College (which later became California State University, Northridge). Frank had been hired at the *Los Angeles Times* around the time that famed *Times* reporter Rubén Salazar was killed on August 29, 1970.

Widespread community reaction to the popular journalist's murder highlighted the need for the media to report on issues relevant to Los Angeles County's large Hispanic population. In 1974 while working at the *Los Angeles Times*, Frank del Olmo met journalism professor Félix Gutiérrez. The two men would later be instrumental in forming a professional organization for Latino journalists.

On-The-Job-Training

I agreed to quickly learn the journalistic skills required of a television reporter. Indeed, within a few months I was working as an investigative journalist, and eventually I became the first Latino television reporter in Los Angeles to focus solely on the Hispanic community.

Those first couple of months at KABC-TV qualified as an accelerated apprenticeship; I had a lot to learn—literally everything about the job. I dutifully followed news reporters Christine Lund and Fred Anderson around for several weeks, and they taught me how to package a story. They would say:

> "Okay, here's what we're doing today. We're covering city hall, where the councilmen [and they were all men] are voting on [a particular issue]. We're going to record brief interviews for and against the proposal. Then we'll go out in the field and interview citizens and/or business owners who will likely be affected by the council's decision."

Critical to the new style of reporting that Bill Fyfe created was to film the reporter on the site taking notes and describing the scene and/or interviewing witnesses. Then the footage would be driven to the station. The film would go in for development and then be returned to us on a big reel that the editor would crank-up so we could see what had been captured by the cameraman.

We would work with the editor to boil the report down to the *Eyewitness News*, story format, which was usually 1 minute and 30 seconds.

I watched my new colleagues cover everything from riots, to court decisions, to community events, and crime scenes. The two months went by quickly, and soon it was time for me to put together my own crew and begin to develop the sources in the community who would lead me to the important stories.

Not much has been written about the obstacles that minority reporters faced during the sixties and seventies. Individuals within the news industry, whether it be newspapers, radio, or television, just didn't like us, and even worse they considered us and our topics irrelevant. Television and motion picture production were especially closed industries—closed to minorities, women behind the camera and anyone who wasn't related or closely tied to an existing AFTRA or SAG member. So, I entered the field without a journalism background, as an outsider, and as a Mexican. News crew members would say, just loud enough for me to hear, "That's not our audience," or "why do we have to drive back to East LA to cover the Mexicans again?"

Even when I could assemble a willing crew, I still had the hurdle of the assignment desk. Although following instructions from the news director to cover the Hispanic community, I had to pitch my stories to the assignment editors, and some were not in sync with the director's views on how news coverage in Los Angeles needed to change to more closely match the demographics of the area. I was regularly criticized for being a "bleeding heart liberal" (which in those days was a real slam in the business world—suggesting that your emotions determined your actions, rather than rational evaluation).

I'm sure I wasn't the only Chicano reporter who had to ignore many nasty racist comments, that in today's legal environment would be completely unacceptable. And not all insults were one-off comments. Indeed, the newsroom nickname for Joe Ramirez and me was "Spic and Span" ("Spic" for Hispanic and "Span" for Spanish).

This is the INS, Open the Door!

Reporters assigned to a news beat must create their own sources and leads as well as investigate stories received from the news services, like the Associated Press. After a time, the public began to know me, and they would call me directly at the station and even on my home phone about stories of interest to Hispanic audiences. I received so many calls, especially about immigration stories. I was called when immigration authorities were staging raids outside churches, schools, and different businesses, especially at the many garment manufacturers in downtown Los Angeles. I'm sure many reporters today are having a similar experience given the current and tragic state of immigration and refugee detention centers around the county.

Reporting from downtown Los Angeles garment district

Covering a labor demonstration in downtown Los Angeles garment district

I was often caught up in raids myself because it was important to "fit in" to get the complete story. Once I was rounded up with others and transported by immigration officers all the way to the federal detention center in downtown Los Angeles where I had to inform the Immigration and Naturalization Service (INS) officers that I was a member of the press. Suffice it to say, I wasn't number one on their list from then on.

When I would arrive with my cameraman and sound technician at a workplace immigration raid, my team and I would be amazed at the scene of people fleeing from the factories and manufacturing plants—running this way and that. I remember asking one of the sweatshop operators why he only employed Mexican workers. He famously said on camera, "I tried white boys and they didn't like the work, and then I tried blacks and they didn't want the jobs either. The Mexicans are just well suited to the work."

During the height of all these raids, we covered one attempted round-up in Long Beach that turned out to be quite humorous. A lady called me and said that she was an apartment manager. Apparently, the INS had been cruising around her complex at different times of the day for several days. She asked me what she should do. I told her that it sounded like they were planning on raiding her complex and that she should plan on accompanying them and unlock the doors to apartments they demanded to enter so that they wouldn't break down the doors. I hoped that she would call me and my crew if the INS entered the two-story complex.

A few days later I got the call at 6:00 a.m. Sure enough, the INS agents were at the apartment complex when I arrived with my crew. They had a list of the apartments they wanted to visit. We followed them to Apartment Number 4 on the first floor. The officers shouted in Spanish, "¡*Agentes de imigración! ¡Abran la puerta! ¡Dónde están sus papeles?*" ("Immigration Service! Open the door. Where are your papers?") After repeating that a couple of times, they asked the manager to unlock the door. She did, and they found the unit empty. We got it all on film. The scene was repeated at Apartment Number 6, with the same result. There was one more attempt on the first floor, and that too resulted in an empty unit.

We followed the officers up to the second floor, where they repeated the process of moving from one suspected apartment to another. We stayed out of their way by staying in front of them but walking backwards along the second-story hallway. As we passed Apartment Number 8, I could see a curtain in the window move slightly. I knew someone was in there and that heightened an already tense situation. Suddenly, the door to Number 8 swung open and there stood a tall Black man in his undershorts, "What the f**k are you talking about?" he yelled. "If memory serves me correctly you're the ones who brought us here 400 years ago and now you want papers! Why don't you get out of here and let a working man get his sleep!" Turns out he had gotten off the late-night shift as a bartender nearby and had just fallen off to sleep when the unsuccessful raid began. Man, he was mad as hell.

I think having done the research on immigration to the Southwestern United States from a historical and economic perspective, I could identify the push/pull economic factors over the last 100 years that enriched my reporting and enhanced audience understanding by being able to see current situations in a historical context. The Southwest workforce had never been large enough to satisfy the burgeoning needs of the production-intensive industries of mining, railroads, agriculture, and automotive, especially in the boom years of the 1920s.

This workforce shortage and high demand for labor coincided with Mexican peasants' need for work following the disruptive Mexican Revolution, which ended in 1920 and after which two million Mexicans had died. Along with thousands of others, it was at that time that my mother's father sent his daughters to Tucson from the state of Sinaloa, México, to be safe from the chaotic conditions. My father left the state of Chihuahua for Tucson about the same time.

Conversely, throughout the 1930s great numbers of excess Mexican workers were forcibly rounded up and repatriated (or deported) following the U.S. stock market crash and subsequent Great Depression. One to two million Mexicans returned to México from Southwestern states. The U.S. Citizen and Immigration Services historical page on the Department of Homeland Security's official website offers a version of 1930 events that counters the more common belief that a federal policy required officers to forcibly remove Mexicans from the Southwest. Rather, it is reported that much of the return to México was self-motivated because of the lack of work during the Great Depression. However, the agency has documented that many state and local governments, often assisted by the Immigration and Naturalization Service (INS), devised deportation programs of their own, none more brutish than in Los Angeles. The program was designed to lessen the burden on Los Angeles area jurisdictions' relief agencies. Shamefully, American citizens were not distinguished from Mexican nationals and hundreds were rounded up in the City of Angels and deported by train. Hispanics were a convenient scapegoat for the 25 percent unemployment rate experienced during the Great Depression.

Describing the situation as a hysterical pandemic deportation in their book, *Decade of Betrayal: Mexican Repatriation in the 1930s,* Francisco Balderrama and Raymond Rodríguez report that some 400,000 Hispanics left the Southwest having been basically forced out by intimidation and employment denial.

Julian Nava, my friend and former U.S. ambassador, former president of Los Angeles Unified School District, and history professor emeritus at Cal State, Northridge, tells the dramatic story of his own family preparing for a deportation date. The family sold all their furniture and any belongings they could not carry, including Julian's mother's much-loved Maytag washing machine and the contents of his father's barber shop. With no work available in 1932, the Nava family, like so many, were assisted by local relief programs. But, like so many Mexican Americans, they were abruptly cut from the relief rolls by Los Angeles County officials. Therefore, even though Julian and his siblings were American citizens, the entire family prepared to repatriate.

In a twist of fate, the Nava family never did leave Los Angeles because young Julian suffered a ruptured appendix on the way to the train station, and he was hospitalized for several weeks. "My family returned from the hospital to pick up the pieces of a demolished life," wrote Nava in his memoir, *Julian Nava: My Mexican-American Journey*. And, pick up the pieces they did. Julian went on to become the first Mexican American to earn a doctorate degree from Harvard University.

Just as the financial paralysis of the U.S. economy began to show some signs of recovery, the U.S. State Department classified Mexicans as "white" in 1937. This determination, combined with the passage of the Nationality Act, which removed barriers to naturalization of Mexicans in 1940, facilitated immigration from México in time for the great need in the United States for factory workers and soldiers as our involvement in World War II seemed eminent, if only at first as a supplier of food and weapons to Britain. We entered the war with a vengeance in December 1941, the day after Japan bombed the U.S. naval station at Pearl Harbor.

In 1942, the United States signed a guest worker program with México called the Bracero Program. The Selective Service Act (the draft) had been re-instated in 1940; and by 1945, 12 million Americans were listed as active duty military personnel. As a result, there was an enormous manpower shortage during World War II, and the Bracero Program provided legal entry for temporary agricultural workers.

The Mexican government viewed the bilateral collaboration favorably because these workers could bring back efficient farming techniques and increase Mexican agricultural productivity. Mexican men who had farming experience were provided transportation by the U.S. government to various farming communities. But because the Mexican government was concerned about possible poor treatment of its citizens while working in the United States, the Bracero agreement contained a provision against transporting the Mexican workers to discrimination prone states. Also, the farm owners were required to pay U.S. farm laborers wages and to provide sanitary housing. The guest workers provided their own food.

Thousands of Mexicans, who did not qualify for the program, but who also needed work, crossed the border to the United States illegally. So many, in fact, that the Bracero Program workers complained that the undocumented Mexican workers drove down their wages. This is a refrain often heard relative to undocumented Mexican workers driving down wages for American workers. Funny, I have yet to meet a student at a U.S. high school or college who strives for back-breaking farming or construction work.

Ironically, just as one government program was pulling immigrants into the United States, another was pushing them out. After World War II, the United States began a new campaign of deportation on a much larger scale than during the Depression. The expulsions, which lasted well into the 1950s, were formalized with the 1954 Operation Wetback (yes, that is the proper title). U.S. authorities arrested and deported more than 1 million people. All in all, the United States sent more than 4 million immigrants, as well as many Mexican Americans, to México, according to the Library of Congress. Interestingly, four million is the same number of temporary farm workers estimated to have participated in the Bracero Program from 1942 to 1964.

Restrictive immigration policies curtailed immigration in 1963, and the Bracero Program was ended in 1964. While the immediate result was an influx of illegal migration, in 1965, 85 percent of Hispanics in the country were born in the United States. Thus, much of the Hispanic community had been victimized by the nearly 50 years of uncertainness of their status in the United States by the time I was hired to introduce their issues to a broader television audience.

Undoubtedly, journalism was in its heyday between 1971 and 1973. Because of what was going on nationally with Watergate and the work of investigative journalists like Bob Woodward and Carl Bernstein, the reporting of Walter Cronkite and Dan Rather from Vietnam, as well as the popular CBS weekly *60 Minutes*, the media was highly regarded by the public. For my part, I felt like I was taking on unjust practices of the immigration service.

Alan Murray was a former agent for the Immigration and Naturalization Service (INS) and the Central Intelligence

Agency (CIA) while I was reporting for KABC-TV. He would give me lots of leads and insight into various forms of corruption. In fact, he gave me a list of 20 or 30 Nazi-era war criminals; three were living nearby in Santa Monica, Seal Beach, and Los Angeles. Alan and his CIA unit had uncovered this. Many of these individuals had been brought into the United States through waivers from congressional representatives, and some to work on scientific projects. Federal agencies looked the other way because the entire space program was initially sourced with many of these folks. I began to report on these individuals, which became quite the scandal because some sitting members of Congress had written the waivers that had exempted the immigrants from prosecution for war crimes. This reporting really put me on the map.

Eyewitness News *anchor Frank Cruz*

Two Stories of National Fascination

In April 1973, White House chief of staff and Nixon loyalist, H.R. (Bob) Haldeman, resigned as the Watergate scandal got too close to the White House. He faced mounting charges that he had masterminded the break-in of Democratic headquarters in the Watergate Hotel in Washington, D.C. He was never convicted of orchestrating the actual break-in, but for his role in the subsequent cover-up he was convicted of perjury, conspiracy, and obstruction of justice. He was sentenced to up to 8 years. Haldeman was released from federal prison after 18 months.

After Haldeman had resigned and before his trial began, the media was anxious to interview him, but he was hiding out. Rumors spread that he may have killed himself. I remembered that, like me, Haldeman had attended USC and, after a stint in the Navy, he had completed his college education at UCLA. I thought if he was a Los Angeles native, maybe his parents still lived there and maybe that was where he had retreated. I found his parents' address in the affluent Hancock Park area of Los Angeles. I got out of the news van and walked right up to the front door and knocked. Unexpectedly, Bob Haldeman himself opened the door and stared silently at me, which I took as my cue.

"Good morning, Mr. Haldeman," I said. "I'm Frank Cruz from KABC-TV. The American public wants to hear from you. Can we have a few minutes of your time?" He took a small piece of paper from his shirt pocket, pulled out a pen, scribbled something on it, handed the paper to me, and shut the door. Wow! This was a real coup; no one in the media could even find this man of national intrigue, and he had written me a note, which I later learned he had taken from Mark Twain's reported 1887 quote after reading his own obituary:

"Reports of my death are greatly exaggerated."

H.R. Haldeman

Not just a few times, the job took on a more dangerous dimension. All Los Angeles television stations are equipped with first-responder radios with someone monitoring the police and fire department communications and the wire services on a 24/7 basis. That person is seated next to the assignment editor who then moves crews around to the various newsworthy events. Just before 2:00 p.m. on May 17, 1974, fellow reporter Christine Lund and I were assigned to follow up on a frantic call for Los Angeles Police Department (LAPD) manpower to surround a small house at the corner of 54th and Compton Avenues, just south of downtown Los Angeles.

Two members of the Symbionese Liberation Army (SLA), who had kidnapped heiress Patty Hearst a year earlier, had been spotted in the area that morning. Police were tipped off by residents in the African American neighborhood about, "those white people with all those guns." This was one of the biggest stories in the nation at the time. People wondered, was Patty really kidnapped? We had all seen the photos of her assisting SLA members with armed bank robberies in Northern California. Had she been brainwashed by this cult? Was she in this house in downtown Los Angeles?

Because of all these unknowns and because of the prominence of the Hearst family name, the cops coaxed and waited, coaxed and waited, calling out more than 20 commands to leave the house. Christine was not a super patient person. When there had been no movement from inside the house, Christine walked right up to the front door and knocked. She was fearless. Luckily for her, the police had been targeting the wrong house and there were no dangerous persons inside.

Christine was a very gutsy reporter but, as events unfolded, she may have realized just how dangerous her walk up to that front door had been.

Once the correct house was identified by the police, a young African American man and a small boy walked out with hands up, but no others. When words didn't work, the LAPD moved to the next step in their Special Weapons and Tactics (SWAT) team protocol, which should have brought the inhabitants out of the house. By about 4:00 p.m., tear gas canisters were being shot into the house. The inhabitants responded to the tear gas with fully automatic gunfire; the cops only had semi-automatic weapons and handguns.

The police were screaming for people to take cover. I remember Christine calling the station for support, "We're going to be down here for a long time," she pleaded. "No, we can't get any closer without getting our heads blown off!"

KABC News reporters Christine Lund and Frank Cruz at SLA shootout in Los Angeles

Christine and I dove under a police car to escape the bullets. This was the closest I ever came to war reporting.

A subsequent review of the incident revealed that more than 9,000 rounds of ammunition had been fired by police and the SLA members. Indeed, many officers had run out of ammunition before the siege had ended. Miraculously, not one bystander (and thousands had converged on the area), police officer, or reporter was injured.

The television coverage of the SLA shootout is reported to have been the first time that an unplanned event was covered live on television nationwide. The whole country was watching the battle, the likes of which Los Angeles had never encountered.

I don't think the police knew exactly who was in that house, and, of course, the overriding concern was that Patty might have been in there. For all anyone knew, SLA Field Marshall Cinque, as he called himself, could have been holding a gun to the heads of his "soldiers" stopping them from surrendering. But the canisters kept flying and eventually caught a curtain on fire, and the little, wood-sided house exploded in flames. By this time many television camera crews were on-site; it was a very chaotic scene with the air polluted by the tear gas, people screaming, and a helicopter flying just above the billowing smoke. In the end, five SLA members died in the fire. Patty Hearst had not been in the house but was apprehended 16 months later in San Francisco.

Learning to Lead

We were breaking barriers, charting untraveled waters, and, more simply put, becoming the first to do many things. I was inspired to help create the country's first professional organization for people of color in journalism. The California Chicano News Media Association (CCNMA) was founded in 1972 by *Los Angeles Times'* writer Frank del Olmo and editor Frank Sotomoyor, KNXT (KCBS) reporter Bob Navarro, KNBC-TV reporter Joe Ramírez, KTTV reporter Joel García, and me. Herman Sillas graciously leant us space in the Los Angeles law offices of Sillas and Castillo, to hold our evening meetings. I was CCNMA's first elected president and served in the role for six years.

California Chicano News Media Association founders, from left: Joe Ramirez, Frank del Olmo, Henry Alfaro, Bob Navarro, and me

The idea of an association emerged from the activism of the sixties. We witnessed the absence of people of color in the media, and we recognized how professional organizations had helped improve diversity among the ranks of doctors and lawyers. We thought we could do the same thing for journalists. The goal was that we would help each other along, network about job opportunities, and foster fair and accurate portrayals of Latinos in the news media. Soon we were joined by Spanish-language reporters, Pete Moraga Sr., Chapo Gómez and a little later by María Elena Salinas.

As the group evolved, we held our meetings during wonderful dinners at La Fonda de Los Camperos, a mid-town Los Angeles restaurant on Wilshire Boulevard, halfway between the Mexican Consulate's office and Mac Arthur Park. I remember a young community activist by the name of Gloria Molina as an up and coming leader of the city speaking at several of those dinners. Gloria Molina would become the first Latina elected to the California State Assembly, the Los Angeles City Council, and Los Angeles County Board of Supervisors.

Back in 1972 and 1973, the value of the CCNMA meetings was to have a simpatico group to bounce ideas off and use as a sounding board for the various dilemmas we encountered during those early days when we were the only people who looked like us on television. Also, the networking was a valuable pipeline for job opportunities about which we would likely not have otherwise been aware.

By 1978 we had received support and funding from the Gannett Foundation, the *Los Angeles Times,* Robert F. Kennedy Foundation, and several media companies. This soon enabled us to provide weekend workshops and scholarships to young Latinos and Latinas studying journalism. We all knew how difficult it was to break into television. Basically, in those days you needed to be related to someone already working in the field to get a spot in the union. The term "old boys' network" doesn't really begin to describe how closely held these jobs were, regardless of whether you were a sound engineer, camera operator, editor, or on-air reporter. Female job seekers were doubly handicapped. Whereas at CCNMA, Andrea Cano was an early leader of the group, as were Estela López and Yvette Cabrera.

Frank Sotomoyor and I were able to coax Professor Félix Gutiérrez out of California State University Northridge to serve as the executive director of CCNMA from 1978 through 1980.

Conversation with Professor Felix Gutierrez

We had been able to construct a full-time job for him in part because of our new relationship with the Gannett Foundation and its Director of Education Jerry Sass. Félix was a tremendous asset to the organization in those early years, and later when he was also a reporter for The Associated Press in its Los Angeles Bureau. Félix was unique among us because he came from a highly educated family in the Los Angeles area. His career in higher education included tenured faculty positions at the University of Southern California (USC) and California State University, Northridge; administrative posts at USC, Stanford University and California State University Los Angeles; as well as a visiting appointment at Columbia University. He retired from USC's Annenberg School for Communication and Journalism as professor emeritus in 2014.

Many young people have entered the field with the help of CCNMA's scholarship program. Awards since 1976 total more than $800,000. For many years the California Chicano News Media Association held an annual scholarship banquet at the Millennium Biltmore Hotel in downtown Los Angeles. Many, already working in the field, have received the prestigious Rubén Salazar Journalism Award for their excellent work published or broadcast in California and contributed to a better understanding of Latinos.

CCNMA also helped spawn the local Asian and Black journalists' associations. Both groups came to us for guidance on how to develop their own organizations. I am especially proud that we were the first.

At a 1982 conference in San Diego, the idea surfaced that a national organization was needed for Chicano journalists. CCNMA's Executive Director Frank Newton suggested that the national group, which in 1984 became the National Association of Hispanic Journalists (NAHJ), borrow the structure and staff that CCNMA had employed successfully. The founders of the NAHJ, including Frank Newton as their director, used CCNMA by-laws and mission statement. In recognition of our work in California, the NAHJ named CCNMA as the sole entrant into its Hall of Fame in 2012.

Chapter Five

I Did the Job Too Well, You Say?

When I was about to reach the three-year mark at KABC-TV, Bill Fyfe called me at home and asked if I could come in for a meeting the next morning. Since my contract was up for renewal soon and because of all the acclaim received for my reporting on immigration issues and the Hispanic community more generally, I was anxious to learn what KABC had in mind for me. We met as usual in his office, right in the middle of the newsroom. I'm embarrassed to say how blindsided I was with the direction of the meeting.

Bill explained that the network had completed "Q Ratings," and based on that data they had conducted some additional focus groups with Los Angeles audiences. The firm Marketing Evaluations in New York compiles the Q Ratings (Q is for quotient, as in IQ), which measures familiarity and popularity of television journalists. It turned out that my face was quite well known to Los Angeles television viewers, which was good, but there was also a downside that I had unknowingly and naively created. Because I had been hired to focus on the Hispanic community and its issues, viewers came to believe that I approached my reporting with a bias. In fact, data from the focus groups showed that many would turn to another channel when my reporting would commence because of this perceived bias.

What a shock! I thought I was doing everything right and reporting the news exceptionally well, only to hear from Bill's own baritone voice, "Yes, you are doing a great job, Frank. And that's the problem." As previously mentioned, he was a man of few words. As directly as I was hired, I learned my contract would not be renewed.

With all humility, I can report that failure, and all its related emotions, had rarely been something I had had to deal with. Well, yes, there was that organic chemistry class. I had made my way through many challenging environments without feeling like a failure. But there I was in Bill Fyfe's office with my emotions running the gamut and back again. For several days, I obsessed on the fact that I had simply done exactly what I had been hired to do. Of course, I shared that with Bill. He understood and agreed, "You're right, Frank. But this is out of my hands. This was a decision made by the network guys in New York."

Once the initial shock began to wear off, I could think beyond KABC-TV and realized that I did have options. I could return to Cal State Long Beach because my leave of absence had not yet expired. I also began to reflect on how the job at KABC had fulfilled my calling to serve the Latino community by bringing their stories and concerns to the forefront and to millions of Southern California living rooms. There's no denying that those three years had been exhilarating and so fundamentally satisfying. As many have said before me, when work aligns with your deeply held values, it doesn't seem like work. That was exactly true for me. I began to hope some good news would come from my agent.

As Luck Would Have It

I should clarify that, I didn't have an agent. I had a "super-agent." Ed Hookstratten was famous in the entertainment and sports world for his representation of Elvis Presley, Johnny Carson, Vin Scully, Pat Riley, Tom Brokaw, and Bryant Gumbel, to name a few. One afternoon at the station, Gumbel had invited me to a party at his house after work. Knowing I was a big Dodger fan, he added that Don Newcomb would be there. No way would I miss a chance to meet the iconic right-hander who, until 2011, was the only pitcher to have won the Rookie of the Year, the Most Valuable Player, and the Cy Young awards.

Sort of in passing. Bryant introduced me to his agent, Ed Hookstratten, at the party. We chatted for a while, and we discovered we were both from the eastside of Los Angeles County, which in those days had a stigma all its own. Ed had gone to Whittier High School and then on to my alma mater USC on a baseball scholarship prior to law school. Ed asked me if I would come to his office in Beverly Hills the following week. In that meeting, Ed explained that he was interested in representing me. Wow! Why me? Honestly, I almost fell off my chair. Ed did add, "First thing, you'll have to cut about a pound of hair off that head if you want to be my client!"

Turned out that in high school Ed's baseball coach was more than just a coach but a mentor who secured him a baseball scholarship at USC. Although Ed's sports career didn't go far (because of an injury, I think), he never forgot the kindness of his Mexican American coach. Ed went on to law school and upon graduation, personal injury attorney Raul Magaña hired him and showed him the ropes of running a privately-owned firm. In our meeting, Ed explained that he had been looking for a way to return the favor of these two Hispanics who had been instrumental in his success. He had decided that representing me was just that opportunity.

Someone once asked me if I believed in luck. My answer was that, while I believe in hard work, I know that there are times and situations that can hardly be described in any other way. What I have learned for sure is to always step up when luck comes knocking. In this case, I did just that, and for the next 10 years Ed Hookstratten's negotiating skills were very helpful to my career and to my young family.

Before I had time to contact California State University Long Beach about returning to the classroom, Ed had a contract for me at KNBC-TV Channel 4 in Los Angeles.

KNBC-TV advertisement for our Emmy Award-winning series

Becoming a More Valuable Employee

Just as I had unwittingly prepared myself by way of a good education and learning as much as I could about broadcasting journalism during those first three years, for the good luck of meeting a super agent who was also from the east side of Los Angeles, I then had to remind myself to be brighter about things this time. I told myself that I needed to become an even better journalist. So, at KNBC-TV I made the decision to continue to do Latino stories but moreover, to concentrate on being a good reporter. My news director assigned me to the Los Angeles Board of Supervisors. The supervisors, including Mike Antonovich, Deane Dana, Ed Edelman, Kenny Hahn, Baxter Ward, and Peter Schabarum, met in the Hall of Administration across the street from the Los Angeles Music Center on the high ground of Bunker Hill in downtown Los Angeles.

I remember a series of hearings that Supervisor Schabarum had called on the popular debate of the day: the drain on society and the burden on county schools, hospitals, and other services created by the growing immigrant population. At one of those hearings, I had the cameras rolling as a series of speakers who were experts on immigration and from various services were painting a very tough picture. I had noticed an elderly lady seated in the middle of the room with her head lowered and a shawl lightly covering her head.

Schabarum was holding court after the presentations. At a slight pause in his tirade, this little woman stood up, letting the shawl fall to her shoulders. “You don’t recognize me, do you, Peter?” she asked. “Please don’t be so hard on these people—your own people. I know you are part Mexican, and you shouldn’t be so hard on your own people.” The room went silent. She gathered her shawl and left the chambers.

Turned out that she had been a neighbor of Pete's while he was growing up. He had turned his back on his roots and she had called him out.

Covering the Courts

Since the supervisors' chambers were just across the street from the court house, I became interested in covering court cases. At the time, the U.S. Attorney's Office and the U.S. Department of Justice were focusing on organized crime in the Southwest, essentially Los Angeles and Las Vegas. The government wanted media coverage of those trials to publicize the administration's tough stance on crime. Normally, it would be somewhat difficult to thoroughly report on both sides of such stories, but in these cases I found the U.S. Attorneys cordial, if not outright helpful in securing publicity for their work. The reason was not necessarily sinister. At different times, different presidents and their administrations have focused on going after particular types of criminal activity, often to prove to the public that campaign promises are being honored.

In an effort to diversify my reporting and become a more valuable asset to NBC, I covered dozens of those "mob" related trials. The allegations were that these offshoots of the crime families in the East were involved in extorting money from clubs and different businesses for "protection on the West Coast." A classic case was a pornography ring that was set up in the San Fernando Valley by the FBI as a sting operation to draw in local criminals tied to the Bonanno family out of New York City and Miami.

I covered so many of those trials that there was a patch of grass lawn outside the court house, which got the nickname "Cruz field" because I summarized outcomes and interviewed plaintiffs and defendants so many times on camera from that patch of grass. I got to know one of the defense attorneys—Howard Weitzman—quite well. Howard even tried to convince me to go to law school, which I did consider for a short while. Howard was always impressed at how current I was on the U.S. Attorneys' cases. Howard has since enjoyed an illustrious career representing the likes of Michael Jackson and his estate, Justin Bieber, O.J. Simpson, Magic Johnson, Morgan Freeman, and Arnold Schwarzenegger. But back then his clients were wise guys like Sam Sciortino, Jimmy "the Weasel" Fratianno, Louis Tom Dragna (known as "The Reluctant Prince"), and Dominic Brooklier (represented by his son Anthony) who became the Los Angeles Mafia Don in 1974 after Nick Licata died.

One morning, while I was in the midst of covering those organized crime trials, Bonnie walked me out to my car parked in the driveway of our Fountain Valley home. She closed the driver's side door and stepped back as I was about to start the car. Bonnie saw something on the ground. She said, "Frank, you're going to want to look at this." I didn't like the tremble in her voice. She had found empty 45 caliber shell casings. I called for a camera crew to document the evidence. Nothing ever came of it, but I definitely considered it a warning.

Reporting on the courts was never boring; it was exciting because you were there with the newsmakers. One day my story might have been tennis great Martina Navratilova, who had been granted political asylum from Czechoslovakia at age 18, receiving her citizenship six years later at the federal court house in 1981. The next day I might have been assigned to the trial of Jimmy "the Weasel" Fratianno from Ohio and his ties to the Eastern crime families.

Another type of criminal activity the Department of Justice was focused on during the early 1980s was the stealing of military secrets, materials, and machinery for buyers in Iron Curtain countries. In particular, I remember FBI agent Howard Miller who fell for a Russian spy. I remember the case because it was part and parcel of all these sales to communist countries. This was before the fall of the USSR and the end of the Cold War, and there were a lot of companies and individuals selling military secrets. The bulk of such activity took place in Los Angeles and San Diego because of the numerous World War II and Cold War military suppliers headquartered near both West Coast ports.

The Department of Justice was interested in news coverage of these cases too. In fact, the U.S. Attorneys had someone in the court who would call to inform me, "Mr. Cruz, at 3:00 this afternoon they're filing an indictment against several individuals. It might be worth your while to come down." That only happened because of the expertise I had developed in covering the courts.

I was often the substitute anchor for the local segment of NBC's *The Today Show*. Reporting on the national news and feature stories would originate in New York and then they would cut away to the local affiliates like KNBC in Los Angeles.

On August 1, 1977, the major story in the Southern California region was a huge fire raging out of control in the Santa Barbara area. We had aerial views of the scene from KNBC's helicopter, piloted by Francis Gary Powers. Years before, Powers had been a civilian pilot flying a CIA spy plane mission over the then USSR.

The U-2 spy plane that Powers piloted, flew at 70,000 feet and was used to surveil Soviet nuclear facilities during the Cold War. Power's plane was shot down and he was captured and interrogated for 107 days before being convicted and sentenced to 10 years hard labor. He was traded two years later for a captured Soviet spy, Rudolf Abel. In 2015, Steven Spielberg made a spy thriller film focused on the negotiations of the swap titled *Bridge of Spies*.

Not only had he had suffered at the hands of the KGB (the main security agency of the Soviet Union), but back home Lt. Powers was ridiculed for not using the poison pin injection device provided to all spy plane pilots in case of their capture. Many Americans thought he should have killed himself.

At the time our news director and general manager at KNBC-TV had been concerned about the possibility of another earthquake, like the disastrous Sylmar quake in 1972, and the inability of our station to adequately cover such a catastrophe. He wanted an "eye in the sky," thus KNBC-TV employed the second "telecopter" in Los Angeles. KTLA had the first TV camera-equipped helicopter in the nation back in 1958. Somehow our general manager also hired this experienced pilot Gary Powers to fly our news chopper and provide footage to augment the weather and traffic reports as well as occasional situations like this giant fire in Santa Barbara County.

I think I was the last person on Earth to speak to Francis Gary Powers.

Powers was assigned that August morning to do live reports on the fire from the chopper at 7, 8 and 9 a.m. At the end of the last segment, I thanked him on air for his coverage. Powers replied on air and said he was low on fuel and heading back to the fueling station. He was never heard from again. The bodies of Powers and cameraman George Spears were found with the crashed chopper in the Sepulveda Dam Recreation Area where Powers attempted to land the chopper using a common emergency procedure for single-engine helicopters called autorotation. Even though the engine is not running, air moves up the rotor system that allows the main rotor to continue turning and providing enough lift for a safe landing. However, Powers made a last second diversion from a safer landing site where he viewed several teenagers playing on a ball field and the helicopter crashed nearby.

Francis Gary Powers was buried at Arlington National Cemetery at the urging of Dick Spangler, president of the Radio and Television News Association of Southern California, and with the approval of President Jimmy Carter.

Fifty years after his capture, Powers' grandchildren were presented with the Silver Star awarded posthumously to their grandfather for "indomitable spirit, exceptional loyalty, and continuous heroic actions while resisting all Soviet efforts through cajolery, trickery and threats of death," reported the *New York Times* on June 15, 2012.

Losing a Dear Colleague

Another favorite colleague was cameraman Bob Brown, the son of a Puerto Rican mother and an African American father. He was very sensitive to Latino issues and filmed many stories with me. Bob went down to Guyana with NBC reporter Don Harris to cover Congressman Leo Ryan's delegation of 18 people to investigate the People's Temple at Jonestown out in the middle of the jungle. "Reverend" Jim Jones had created this cult, preying on many people, especially blacks. Prior to the compound in Guyana, his People's Temple had been in Congressman Ryan's district in the San Francisco area, where several of his constituents had sought his help, out of concern for family and friends who were involved with the cult.

When allegations of Jones' fraud, associated with his congregants' welfare and pension payments, were percolating up to law enforcement, he moved all 900 men, women, and children to Guyana in South America. In preparation for a possible raid by local authorities, Jones had required the entire group to practice mass suicide, more than once, by drinking supposedly poisoned "Kool-Aid" after serving it to the little ones.

On November 18, 1978, the congressman's visit began pleasantly enough. But then several people began handing him notes and making pleas (when they could not be heard) to take them back to California. Indeed, 16 Jones' followers returned to the Port Kaituma airstrip with the delegation at the end of the day's visit. As they began boarding the plane, a jeep pulled up and several armed men began shooting. Cameraman Bob Brown began shooting too. His weapon was his camera. He was documenting their attempt to escape out of the jungle until he fell. In the end, five people were murdered there: Congressman Leo Ryan; reporter Don Harris; a photographer for Hearst Newspapers; soundman Steve Sung; and my friend, Bob Brown.

Survivors dragged themselves and other wounded off the airstrip and into the jungle. Several hours later, when it seemed that the assassins would not return, Don Harris' producer, Bob Flick, a couple of NBC photographers, Bob Brown's sound man Steve Sung, *Washington Post* reporter Charles Kraus, and Congressman Ryan's aide Jackie Speier boarded the plane with their slain colleagues and headed for the United States.

Local authorities learned of the massacre at the airstrip and proceeded to the encampment to investigate. When they arrived the next day, they found the dead bodies of 909 people, including Jones himself, decomposing in the tropical heat. Two hundred were children who had been fed the Kool-Aid-like drink, reportedly by their parents. Others were injected in the back with cyanide and a few died from gunshot wounds.

The assumption was that many, including all the children, were murdered and many more voluntarily, committed suicide. Outside of war, this was the worst American tragedy, that had occurred up to that time. I'm not sure if people today using the phrase, "they've drunk their own Kool Aid," actually know the source of their reference to this most horrendous result of group think and, mind control in U.S. history.

I had been at KNBC for about four years when my good friend Bob Brown died at Jonestown doing his job. The large attendance at his funeral in Hollywood honored the man and his profession.

Opportunities Abound for the Bi-lingual

I'll just say it. I love the Los Angeles Dodgers. In fact, when the O'Malley family offered the team for sale in 2015, I joined a consortium of business people who made a very competitive bid for the team. Time will tell if the group fronted by Magic Johnson will have been good for the team or not. But back in 1981, as a reporter, I got the thrill of a lifetime.

The Dodgers had just signed a young pitcher from Etchohuaquila, Sonora, México. He won his first eight games; the first five were shutouts. Los Angeles was overcome with "Fernandomania." Fernando Valenzuela is the only major league player to win both the Rookie of the Year and Cy Young awards in the same season. In 1986, he was also awarded the Golden Glove. KNBC-TV's sportscaster at the time, and for many years, was Canadian Stu Nahan. Stu came over to me one day in the studio, and asked, "Frank, how the hell do we get this guy on television?" Fernando could not speak English and Stu spoke no Spanish. Here you had a kid from México—I guess the Dodgers had had a scout down in México who discovered him—and he was causing a frenzy in Los Angeles. The fans had nicknamed him "The Bull" and demanded that the ABBA song "Fernando" be played every time Valenzuela took to the pitcher's mound.

I suggested to Stu, "Let's try to bring him in on an off day for the team and sit him up with you. I can sit between you, but a little behind, and I can translate your questions and his answers." Believe it or not, that had never been done before in the United States. The positive reaction, especially in Los Angeles, was fascinating. The national news media were watching too. We tried things that just weren't common business practices at the time.

Surprise, Surprise, there is News South of the Border

Unimaginable today, but up to that point in the early 1980s no one in the broadcast media had ever covered Mexican politics. I did; I was the first. The major political parties in México are the PRI and the PAN. Prior to the catastrophic earthquake that would devastate México City in 1985, I had convinced the KNBC people that the Mexican presidential elections of 1986 would be of great interest to Southern California viewers. I travelled throughout México, visiting numerous states. I walked the streets and interviewed voters and covered the campaigning and the elections.

Finding colleagues at KNBC to cover stories of interest to the Hispanic community had taken some time. Superior reporting requires a small but experienced and creative team. As a minority, when you get in to these big organizations you get to know who would be supportive. In my case, I needed the technical people, such as cameramen, producers, and editors who might also be sensitive to certain topics. You might say my antennae were always up for opportunities to forge those relationships and continue serving the Hispanic community.

One such project was particularly rewarding. I won an Emmy in the documentary category for a week-long special that ran every day during the prime-time newscast during sweeps week in 1982. During sweeps, networks roll out the big guns, such as spectacular episodes of sitcoms and the like, to inflate viewership, which loosely translates to the rates they can charge advertisers for the upcoming months. More viewers equal higher advertising prices that equal more revenue for the network.

Ruben Norte, a Mexican American from El Paso, Texas, worked as a producer and a news writer at KNBC. Ruben and I pitched our idea for a week-long special titled *The Latinization of Los Angeles*. We were allotted a crew and we covered six major topics with five- to six-minute reports: history, immigration, education, demographics, cultural realities, and politics. The series aired in May 1982 and got a lot of reaction in the journalism world in Southern California and across the country. People were saying, "Look at this Mexican journalist. Look what he's doing and how he's covering the community and its issues." Although the topics were basically the same as those covered in the earlier Chicano heritage television series that I hosted 12 years before, these reports were being shown during prime time, filmed on location, and produced with a professional technical crew.

One day we were out in the U.S.-México border area talking to the people smugglers, or *coyotes*. The next day we might have been shopping in downtown Los Angeles' Grand

Central Market buying food items that many television viewers had probably never heard of. We also filmed at historic sites, including the ancient ruins of the Aztec empire in México.

Talking with coyotes and others looking to cross into the U.S.

Reporting from the Calexico border

Reporting from Los Angeles Grand Central Market

The 15 years I spent between these two major-market, network stations might serve as a cautionary tale to journalism students who will experience trials and tribulations with limited funds, limited personnel, and prohibitive technology costs. But for those with a driving force, such as mine, to share the Latino story, or any other selfless motivations, a good outcome can result. As it turned out, I had to move on from in front of the camera to behind it to reach my highest potential. Learning every step of the way, always with my antennae up for new aspects of the craft and the business, appreciating my mentors, as well as stepping up to every opportunity or stroke of luck, built an unlikely and very fulfilling career in television news.

One September morning on my way from our Fountain Valley home to the KNBC-TV studios in Burbank, I received a call on the two-way radio we used in those days. The news director told me not to bother even coming upstairs to my desk when I arrived, but as soon as I could get out of my car, he wanted me in a waiting limo that would take me and a small crew to the Burbank Airport (now the Bob Hope Airport). I learned that one of the last stories I would do for KNBC, and one of the most impactful ones, was leading the first U.S. news team to the scene of the devastating 1985 earthquake in México. At 5:30 that morning, I had heard about the quake on the radio, but I had no idea that I would be arriving in México City in just a few hours. A Lear jet was waiting for us at the airport, and we headed to México to cover the aftermath of the 8.0 magnitude quake, the worst ever to rock that country. The impact was amplified by the geophysical phenomenon called soil liquefaction.

The earthquake's epicenter was off the Pacific coast in the Middle America Trench. But miles away, México City had been built on the ancient lake bed of Lake Texcoco with sandy soil always saturated by a high-water table. As this earthquake caused the ground to vibrate, the soil particles lost contact with one another and the solid ground behaved like a liquid. Just as the word suggests, and as scientists described the condition, the ground basically turned to jelly. The violent waves continued much longer than in a "normal" earthquake, and the ground could no longer support the weight of the city's buildings.

Because the word was that no runways were open at Benito Juárez International Airport, we were planning to land in Toluca, rent a car, and drive the 60 miles into México City. Suddenly the pilot, who did not speak Spanish, asked me to come up and translate a transmission from the control tower at Benito Juárez. The frantic speaker was saying that they believed Runway #1 was safe for landing. That's all we needed to hear. Being the first on a scene like this would be important to our viewers since so many had strong ties to México. It would also be important to local and network ratings, since our coverage would be aired nationally.

As we approached the city limits, none of us were prepared for the devastation below. Building, after building had collapsed on itself. After landing, we rented a *combi*, a VW wagon, and headed for downtown between 1 or 2 o'clock in the afternoon. The earthquake had hit at 7:19 a.m. (5:19 a.m. Los Angeles time). Today, news of large earthquakes is broadcast immediately around the globe, but this was before Ted Turner's Cable News Network. Due to the tragic scene, we knew we were going to be staying a while and needing a hotel, preferably one that was still standing.

We dropped off the camera and sound crew at the Plaza Hotel, which could only accommodate two of us, and drove around the block to another. The second hotel's registration desk was at the end of a huge walkway. I checked in and asked the attendant where the gift shop was. Having had no notice of the assignment or its duration when I left the house that morning, I knew I would need some things—a razor for one. Just at that moment, a 7.5 aftershock hit the city with the same liquefaction-enhanced intensity and duration.

I had experienced several earthquakes in my 20 years in California, but never anything like this. I did what the experts tell you not to do; I ran out of the lobby. I also think I picked up three religions and atoned to anyone I had ever hurt along the way. The shaking stopped and started up again during what was the longest 30 seconds of my life.

Our photographer had run out into the street too. I yelled, "Let's get back into the van and get some footage so we can get something through to New York, pronto!" We drove to the other hotel to find the sound man ready to go. But Willis, our cameraman, was sitting on the curb with his head in his hands. I walked over to him, he looked up and said, "Frank, God is talking to me."

"Yeah, this is awful," I replied, "but come on, let's get your camera and start to work."

"Frank, you don't understand. God is talking to me," Willis repeated.

Willis had been sitting on the toilet in his 14th- floor room when the aftershock hit. The force literally blew the bathroom wall off the building and onto the street 150 feet below. He pulled up his pants, made the treacherous run down the 14 flights of stairs that were surely heaving one way and then the other. Willis was now huddled on the curb, his camera abandoned in his room.

Willis was a veteran cameraman. I had worked with him on numerous assignments, but something snapped that day. I tried to coax him out of his anxiety-driven delirium by reminding him that he would be penalized and fined by the network and his union if he didn't get to work. I spent all the time I thought I could, but I was never successful. He just kept repeating, "God is talking to me." Indeed, he did eventually make his way to the airport and caught the first plane back to California.

We found a local freelance cameraman who worked out great because he also knew how to navigate the city. Although the broadcast tower for the largest mass media production company in the Spanish-speaking world, Televisa, had crumbled to the ground, we were happy to see the public broadcasting TV Azteca's tower was still standing. So, we knew we would be able to send our footage to New York via Azteca. As the first international reporters on the scene, we began transmitting footage to the States.

The next day, we followed the rescue dogs and their handlers through the rubble. The dogs were all breeds and were so impressive. The handlers would send them into what was left of a collapsed building. If the dogs came out wagging their tails it meant someone was alive in the wreckage. If tails were not wagging, the dogs evidently had smelled death.

The 12-story Juárez Hospital had collapsed and 750 people who were trapped had died in the rubble. The devastation at the hospital was brutal. I had never seen anything like that before. However, many days into the rescue efforts, the dogs found several newborn babies still alive though they had been buried for 9 days—their entire lives. The right hands of rescuers and observers, like my crew, furiously fashioned the sign of the cross on our chests, having witnessed what could best be described as a miracle. I've often wondered if these children have enjoyed two birthday celebrations each year since—once on September 19 and again 9 days later.

Chapter Six

Doc's Magic

My delicate interviews with plaintiffs and my daily coverage of the Madrigal v. Quilligan court case in 1978 had been a painful experience. Yet in so many ways, this was the most important of all the court proceedings I covered in my 15 years as a television news reporter in Los Angeles.

I had learned of the case in about 1974 when young UCLA law school graduate Antonia Hernández called me to share information she had received from Dr. Bernard Rosenfield, a resident intern at Los Angeles County General Hospital. Rosenfield had provided Antonia, and the East Los Angeles legal aid organization she was working for, with copies of files on nearly 200 women who, the maternity ward records showed, had been sterilized immediately following giving birth or during Cesarean section deliveries. The medical files also revealed that most of the women could not read English and therefore didn't know what was being planned for them, but they had signed consent forms based on their trust in the doctors and nurses who were treating them during their deliveries.

I took the information directly to Bill Fyfe, my news director at KABC-TV. Bill assigned me to report on the back story leading up to the trial. Four years later, I covered each day of the 1978 trial while working for KNBC-TV.

The poignant plaintiffs' testimony was shared with the television audience. The women described how each of them had been admitted to Los Angeles County General Hospital's maternity ward, and while experiencing the multiple stressors of childbirth, a language barrier, and sedation effects, each had been tricked into agreeing to a sterilization procedure as a postscript to giving birth.

"Do you want the pain to end? Sign here," she was told. "Would you like a tubal ligation? Sign here." "Your husband has already agreed to the second procedure. Sign here."

We also reported on the tragic cases in which young doctors, needing surgical experience, sterilized women who spoke no English and who had never understood why they could never get pregnant again. That is until the lawyers putting together the Madrigal class action lawsuit against the hospital sought them out and explained what the doctors had done to their bodies. Imagine the anger and humiliation they must have felt when they learned the truth.

While in Judge Jesse William Curtis Jr.'s U.S. district courtroom in downtown Los Angeles, I listened to testimony from one of two medical professionals who spoke against Dr. Edward James Quilligan, who was the lead defendant and had been the head of obstetrics and gynecology at County General since 1969. The witnesses quoted Dr. Quilligan as having shared his related philosophy in a department meeting: "Poor minority women in L. A. County are having too many babies; it is a strain on society, and it is good that they be sterilized."

I was also present to hear Judge Curtis' unfathomable ruling in favor of the hospital and against the plaintiffs. Over the years many people have asked me how something like this was possible in California.

Many young people know the state only for its current progressive political leanings. But going back to the early 1900s, Californians had been very supportive of a faulty science called eugenics. The commonly held, indeed worldwide, belief was that a variety of maladies, such as mental illness, blindness, criminal, and other degenerate behavior, such as laziness, were passed on from parents to their offspring. Therefore, it followed that a scientific remedy was to stop anyone afflicted with these problems from bringing more of their kind into the world.

In its most evil expression, eugenics was the "science" that ultimately lead to Hitler's "cleansing" of the Aryan race during World War II. Once the Nazi propaganda machine had succeeded in dehumanizing the Jewish people, the regime was able to shift the nation's fear of Germany's serious financial problems after World War I to a loathing of the other—Jews.

In the United States in 1909, California had been the third state to pass a law allowing the unwanted "asexualization" of inmates and patients, if such a procedure "would improve their behavior." California's secretary of the State Commission on Lunacy (yes, really) went so far as to promote the sterilization of patients in the care of the state.

It seems natural that people appalled by the outcome in the Madrigal v Quilligan case often speculate on a different outcome had a decision rested with a jury rather than Judge

Curtis alone. I must admit to having been surprised when it was announced that Judge Curtis was going to sit on the bench in this case, since he was quasi retired at the time. I had covered trials with many different federal court judges. There was Judge Terry Hatter, Judge Andrew Hauk, Judge Wallace Tashima, and Judge William Byrne, and many others who were there in the courts on an active basis.

Sadly, I'm not so sure a jury trial would have resulted in a different outcome. You see, sterilization without consent was viewed, by not just a few, as the appropriate antidote to a nation's ills. Having knowledge of the 1920's prevailing and faulty science of eugenics, and with the benefit of hindsight, it is easier to understand society's misguided need to focus on scapegoats during the Great Depression and thereafter. Weren't the poor, the disabled, the newly immigrated, and the otherwise disenfranchised the source of the nation's problems? Indeed, by the end of the decade, as the country and, soon, the entire western world, fell into the Great Depression, the need to shift from fear of the future intensified as did blame on "the other."

So even with the evidence of how eugenics beliefs, aided by a skillful propaganda machine, were used by the Nazis against the Jewish people in the 1930s and 1940s, in the 1960s our country was clutched by many fears over which the average citizen had seemingly no control. The overarching fear of nuclear war with USSR, the anguish caused by the murder of beloved political leaders, and the emerging science of ecology and its warnings of the consequences of overpopulation were all top of mind in the U.S.

To lock down the lid on this pressure cooker were the unintended consequences from President Lyndon Johnson's 1964 declaration of a "war on poverty." Offering health care coverage for the first time to the poorest U.S. citizens was a hallmark of his proposals. However, Medicaid rules unwittingly incentivized physicians and struggling public hospitals and prison sick bays to inflict harm on those with very little social clout. Medicaid provided a 90 percent reimbursement for the costs associated with performing sterilization procedures. In California, hysterectomies and tubal ligations increased 742 percent from 1968 to 1969 alone.

Overall, unwanted sterilizations were imposed on some 60,000 persons in the United States—20,000 of those surgeries were perpetrated against California residents.

Covering this trial was my introduction to two brave young women who were to become iconic champions of justice for Mexican Americans, especially related to women's issues.

Women's health advocates from the community action group the Comision Femenil Mexicana Nacional and legal counsel Antonia Hernández located a handful of Latina victims. Founders Gloria Molina, Olivia G. Rodríquez, and Evelyn V. Martínez had searched out the core of the class action plaintiffs against the hospital and its administrators. Antonia Hernández came to me to see if I could devise a method of recording the stories of these women who did not want to be on camera, at least in those early days of the developing case. Antonia had seen the many reports I did on Latino issues. I often conducted interviews in Spanish and translated both questions and answers for English-speaking viewers. I had developed a reputation for being sensitive to issues of the Hispanic community. I think that is why Antonia Hernández reached out to me.

In a phone call to me, Antonia also encouraged me to cover the upcoming class action lawsuit with the hope that

I could also interview the victimized women. Arrangements were made for me and a cameraman to visit the women who were very shy and deeply humiliated by the assault of the doctors upon their bodies.

In addition to being able to speak to the Latinas in Spanish, as a reporter I had learned how to put people at ease and to create a bond of sorts by using good listening skills along with body language and tone of voice that were congruent with my words. These interpersonal skills conveyed my authentic caring and respect for the people I interviewed.

I decided to physically arrange each interviewee with her back to the camera because none wanted their identities exposed to the community and, in some cases, especially not to family members, many of whom did not know anything at all about the procedures performed at County General Hospital.

The coordination of those heartfelt interviews and my coverage of the trial are the basis for a lifelong friendship and professional relationship with both Antonia Hernández and Gloria Molina.

Throughout her decades as a legal defense attorney and later as president and CEO of the Mexican American Legal Defense Fund (MALDEF), Antonia and I worked together many, many times. Her cases were often at the heart of the Latino community. Surprisingly, over the years we never discussed having started our academic careers at East Los Angeles College or of the mentorship we each had enjoyed from Social Sciences Department Chair Helen Miller Bailey (1909–1976).

Similarly, over the years I reported on the political career of young community organizer Gloria Molina as she moved through the ranks to become the first Latina to serve as a Los Angeles County Supervisor. I remember arranging for her to speak at several CCNMA dinner meetings. And yet I had never known she had attended ELAC as a part-time student who enrolled in evening classes taught by "Doc Bailey," as the professor was known on campus.

Not until about 2010 was it discovered by my co-author Rita Soza that no less than six former students and devotees of Helen Miller Bailey had been in some way involved in the Madrigal v Quilligan case. In her research for the Helen Miller Bailey biography, Soza probed us for events that we felt had been significant or turning points in our careers. Initially, only Rita became aware that all of us claimed Helen Miller Bailey as our mentor and separately would additionally cite our involvement with this court case as a pivotal point in our careers.

Antonia recalled that after graduating from ELAC she enrolled at California State University Los Angeles. She added that it was Helen who encouraged her to reach a little higher and submit an application to UCLA. Antonia would later tell Rita that Helen Miller Bailey had been "the greatest influence on my life." The two women became great friends, and Antonia has relayed with sadness the many hours she spent reading to the old professor who succumbed to side effects of experimental cancer treatment in 1976. Antonia Hernández has served as president and CEO of the California Community Foundation since 2004.

One of Soza's interviewees suggested she also contact Los Angeles County Supervisor Gloria Molina in connection with the Bailey biography. Molina spoke of being mesmerized in Doc Bailey's classes. As a shy, young Latina who had just begun to consider formulating a professional presence, Molina admitted she tried to emulate Doc's energetic spirit, positive attitude, and engaging eye contact.

Molina went on to explain, "Helen Miller Bailey served as a type of role model that few of us had in our lives. She made you want to be some body and she actually served as the pathway to significant work in service to our community and state."

Gloria Molina went on to a groundbreaking career in electoral politics. In a twist of fate, a quarter of a century after the Madrigal trial, Los Angeles County Supervisor Gloria Molina would oversee the construction of a new Los Angeles County/University of Southern California Medical Center, where the prior abuses had taken place.

As the Madrigal case was being developed, Antonia Hernández enlisted the help of UCLA law school student Richard Àvila. Together they composed the 1976 *UCLA Chicano Law Review* article, "Chicanas and the Issue of Involuntary Sterilization: Reforms Needed to Protect Informed Consent." Àvila also contributed to supplemental legal briefs to Judge Curtis.

In 2006, a librarian at Helen Miller Bailey's namesake library at ELAC suggested Soza interview the same Richard Àvila who, "might have known Doc Bailey." Indeed, Àvila had enjoyed a long friendship with his professor, first as her student and teacher's assistant, then as a member of the Mexican American Students Association (MASA) with Doc Bailey serving as the faculty sponsor. Years later Àvila spent hours at Helen's bedside in her last days.

Richard Àvila graduated from the UCLA School of Law and went on to serve as deputy California attorney general, health quality enforcement, for 12 years, after which he returned to ELAC to teach history for many years. Richard once shared with Soza, "I guess Helen got her way after all. She always wanted me to become a teacher." Upon retirement from teaching, Àvila fulfilled a life-long dream of volunteering for the Peace Corps.

I've already described the impact Doc Bailey had on the direction of my academic career. Due to her professional generosity and boundless energy, she and I were able to develop the first secondary educational textbook to focus on Latin Americans and their (our) relationship to the development of the United States. Because of that text, I became known as a Latin American scholar, which led to inclusion in that first television series, *Chicano I and II*, and ultimately lead to me being asked to become a reporter covering the Latino community in Los Angeles. That first job at KABC-TV was the start of my rewarding career in the media. Clearly, maintaining my friendship with Doc Bailey fostered our academic collaboration that was a pivotal chapter in my life.

In 2015, Antonia, Gloria, and I were all interviewed at the premiere special screening of the documentary recounting the Madrigal case. The PBS, Emmy-nominated documentary, *No Más Bebés*, was written by Virginia Espino and directed by Renee Tajima-Peña.

If you live in California, you might be wondering now where we stand relative to the 1909 (coincidentally the year of Doc Bailey's birth) decision for California to become the third state to legalize the sterilization of patients and inmates. That question can only be answered by introducing another former Helen Miller Bailey student.

In 1979, California State Assemblyman and Chairman of the Assembly's Health Committee Art Torres introduced a bill to repeal the state's sterilization law. Torres' bill was unanimously approved in the State Assembly and then in the Senate. The 1909 law was repealed in 1983.

Journalism professor Félix Gutiérrez and the role he has played in the advancement of Latino journalists at CCNMA was presented in a previous chapter. But what was not revealed was that upon graduating from high school in 1961, Gutiérrez was selected to receive an Armando Castro Scholarship administered by Helen Miller Bailey to help with first year college expenses at Los Angeles State College. Félix Gutiérrez retired in 2014 from the University of Southern California as journalism professor emeritus.

In 2008, Sociology Professor Elena R. Gutiérrez authored, *Fertile Matters, The Politics of Mexican Origin Women's Reproduction*, which is one of the first scholarly accounts of the Madrigal case. I was proud to offer her some support with her important endeavor.

Included in her biography of Helen Miller Bailey, and during various public speaking events, Soza has revealed that not only was she a former student of Professor Bailey, but more importantly, and previously unbeknownst to us, those Chicana/o leaders who with others are responsible for repealing the law in 1983 that had for more than 70 years sanctioned the nonconsensual sterilizations of Californians were all students of Professor Helen Miller Bailey, Ph.D. at East Los Angeles College.

In one form or another, Antonia Hernández, Gloria Molina, Richard Àvila, Art Torres, Félix Gutiérrez, Rita Joiner Soza, and I shared the support and mentorship of a great professor.

All of us have agreed that Helen Miller Bailey had a way of connecting the right people with the right opportunities. She had the unique ability to identify our academic and professional potential, which at the time was quite hidden from our own view.

Although we all have become friends and colleagues in pursuit of equity for Mexican Americans, none of us had really been prepared to learn in later years that Helen Miller Bailey is the connection that drew us to each other—what we have all come to call "Doc's magic."

In 2014, East Los Angeles College completed a renovation of Helen's namesake library. As her biographer, Rita Soza helped with planning the event and bringing several of us together to participate in the celebration.

Antonia Hernández, Julian Nava (also a Bailey devotee), Rita Soza, and me at the Helen Miller Bailey Library re-dedication ceremony

Catching up with Armida Avila at Helen Miller Bailey Library celebration

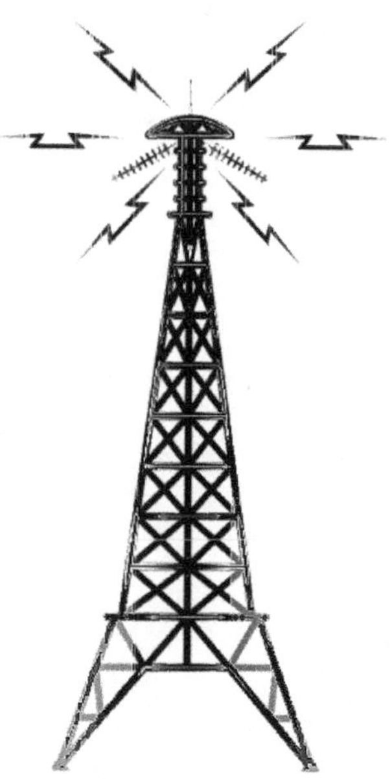

Part III

Chapter Seven

Stepping Back Behind the Camera

In addition to the investigative reporting I was doing at KNBC-TV from 1975 to 1985, I anchored the weekend news for several years. I anchored on Saturday and Sunday and then worked as a field reporter for three days during the week. Often, especially when sweep week was over, Jess Marlow would take several days off and I would be asked to fill in for the prime-time anchor. We broadcast the *News at 5*, which was a one-hour show broken up into the news, weather, sports, and a closing. After that broadcast, we were off air for a couple of hours. During that time, we would film a few 20-second, upcoming news teasers, which would be shown between 6:00 and 10:00 p.m. Then we'd come back with an updated version of the hour newscast at 11:00 p.m.

These longer substitution gigs were whetting my appetite for the next logical move in my television news career. I set my sights on a prime-time, weekday anchor chair.

KNBC weekend news anchor team

My agent was very persuasive. I was told that network executives would cringe at the thought of having to negotiate with Ed Hookstratten. Each time there was an opening, I would express my interest and Ed would follow up with a meeting with network management. One of those anchor spots went to John Beard from North Carolina in 1981. The next opening went to another Anglo reporter, whose name escapes me. For all the positives that occurred at KNBC-TV, what was beginning to grate on me was that I wanted to be a full-time, prime-time anchor. When they hired Beard, I asked Ed to find out the real reason I was passed over. All he was told was that it was a decision out of New York and out of the hands of the local station management. That wasn't much of an answer.

I was looking for some coaching that would ensure a future promotion. I told myself there would surely be other opportunities. They must be happy with me or I wouldn't be the

fill-in guy, right? And, after all, I had just earned a Golden Mike award for KNBC in 1983 as the news anchor for a 4:00 p.m. broadcast with my co-anchor, Tritia Toyota. So, when the next anchor spot came up, Ed negotiated hard on my behalf. The negative result really caused me to contemplate a limited future in front of the camera. NBC ultimately filled that opening with Nick Clooney, actor George Clooney's dad, from Cincinnati.

I wasn't happy, but one of my most helpful personal traits has always been resiliency. You see, at that point in my career at KNBC, most rejections, disparaging remarks, and negative attitudes I encountered in my 13 years as a Latino reporter in a white and incestuous industry had served as a catalyst for me to work harder and to be more innovative to prove the naysayers wrong. But this was too much. What did some guy from Ohio know about the greater Los Angeles community?

For a few days, my emotions traversed from disappointment to anger and back again. I'd been anchoring for Jess Marlow and John Shubeck and they gave the spot to someone else! What was up with that? Then it hit me one day; the Nick Clooney hire had made it clear. If they couldn't make me an anchor, what was the future? My belief in a career as a full-time, prime-time, television news anchor was sinking (pun intended).

I will admit to having moments when a typically silent (by then) inner critic would shout out:

Maybe you're not really cut out for this.

Maybe you should simply be proud of how far you have come from Barrio Hollywood.

This is it, accept that you've reached the height of your career.

During these brief but intense moments, I began to think that maybe the classroom was where I really belonged.

Ultimately, KNBC-TV management explained that "corporate" in New York had a formula that was working around the country. They were pairing a seasoned (white—my observation) male anchor with a young female reporter. Clooney could have been paired with reporters Kelly Lange or Tritia Toyota or Kirsty Wilde, I don't really remember, and it really didn't matter. I began to focus on my exit strategy.

That summer of 1985, I met Joe Wallach, a retired network executive with CBS. We became instant friends and got together many times. Because of his recent success in television broadcasting in Brazil, the topic of our conversation often drifted to the status of Spanish-language television in the Los Angeles area. Though we approached the subject from different perspectives, we always came to the same conclusion.

Joe viewed broadcasting by Los Angeles' only Spanish-language station, KMEX-TV, from the technical perspective of someone who had started an international television network, TV GLOBO in Brazil.

I approached the content from the point of view that the Spanish-speaking community deserved another option. You only had to examine the 1970 and 1980 census data to see how the population of Los Angeles was growing and the demographics shifting. And you only needed to listen to the concerns of community leaders to know that local coverage of the community deserved expansion.

We agreed that what KMEX was offering at the time was not good enough.

As I said, Joe and I had connected right away. He shared details of what he had done for Time Life Broadcasting Corporation which owned the CBS television station in San Diego and in Brazil. I wanted to know how he had ended up in Brazil from San Diego. As he told it, he was in the middle of a nasty divorce during his last years as general manager of the CBS affiliate KOGO-TV in San Diego. His news anchor was Regis Philbin and his weather reporter a young Raquel Welch. Joe told me that to keep his sanity throughout his divorce proceedings he approached the Time Life executives for a transfer "as far away from San Diego as possible." They took him at his word, and before long he was managing a station in Rio de Janeiro, Brazil.

Joe discovered the dreadful, or should I say, basically nonexistent condition of media coverage in the country. He learned that there were plenty of Brazilians living in the countryside who didn't even know that the town of Brasilia had been established as the capital of the country in 1960, much less where it or other metropolitan centers, such as Rio de Janeiro or São Paulo were even located. Joe saw a need and an opportunity. On behalf of Time Life, he created the fourth-largest television network in the world in 1980 and used television to unify a nation. Those who can read Portuguese can delve into the details as described in Joe's autobiography, *Meu Capítulo Na TV Globo (My Chapter in TV Globo).*

Joe was excited about the potential of the Hispanic advertising market in Los Angeles. Lucky for me, I could rattle off the numbers because not long before I had done extensive research for the 1982 Emmy-winning series, *The Latinization of Los Angeles.* The numbers spoke for themselves—there was definitely a business case for a second, full-time Spanish-language television station in Los Angeles.

Joe had a proven track record in the industry, and I had the local expertise. The idea began to surface that we could run a station ourselves if we could get our hands on one. Joe started asking around and, serendipitously, a basically dormant Channel 52 FCC license was offered for sale by Oak Industries' principals Larry Perenchio and Norman Lear. This UHF station offered pay-for-view sporting events. Joe was on vacation in Brazil when he found out about a possible financing opportunity for Channel 52. He contacted Reliance Capital Group and its chairman Saul Steinberg (known for hostile takeovers), which kicked off a series of meetings in New York.

Together we made a compelling pitch. The Reliance people knew that they would be buying talent. Joe's immense success in Brazil was very intriguing to them. The demographic data that would translate to advertising sales was all in my head from having done the research. They matched up my information with that of the big advertising agencies like Foote, Cone, and Belding in Chicago and local agencies like the Orci Agency in Los Angeles. I can't explain how excited the investors were to hear the numbers.

Our idea to purchase Channel 52 was also supported by a technological advantage. In the Los Angeles basin, most of the television channels—2, 5, 7, 9, 11, and 13— broadcast in VHF (very high frequency) format. However, Channels 52 and 34 (KMEX) broadcast in the lower power UHF (ultra-high frequency). But with new technology, the UHF signal could be amplified to increase audience reach to match that of the VHF stations. Advertisers in New York and Chicago had recently been responding to the advantages of UHF amplification in large markets like Los Angeles.

Additionally, looming in the background were some reports that were beginning to surface, from media scholars like Félix Gutiérrez, that the ownership of KMEX-TV was in some legal jeopardy. The station had been founded in 1961 by Mexican media baron, Emilio Azcárraga and those with connections to him in México. United States law limited foreign ownership of domestic television and radio stations to 20 percent, and from the reports it seemed that there could likely be some level of disruption at KMEX Channel 34.

In November 1985, the Reliance Capital Group became our partner and put together $30 million ($70 million in today's money) to purchase the dormant Channel 52 FCC license and revive its offices and production studio. Joe and I had our own station!

The source of funding was Michael Milken from Drexel Burnham Lambert (DBL). Milken had moved the DBL high-yield bond operation to Los Angeles in 1978, thus we were in some amazing company. For those who want to learn more about Michael Milken, I recommend Connie Bruck's book, *The Predators*, in which she details how Milken financed such businesses as Ted Turner's CNN, home builders KB Homes and Toll Brothers, cell phone pioneer Craig McCaw, Steve Wynn Resorts, Larry Ellison's Oracle, and Bill McGowan's MCI international fiber-optic network.

Joe and I renamed the station KVEA-TV ("*vea*" is Spanish for "see"). The studio was in Glendale, just northwest of Los Angeles, in a complex adjacent to the old Grand Central Airport. In fact, every time *Casablanca*, is aired on Turner Classic Movies, I always look forward to the final airport scene when Humphrey Bogart pulls a switch on Ingrid Bergman, explaining that she will be leaving on the plane with her husband, and it will be Bogie who will be staying behind. The acting is very dramatic, but I focus on the foggy scene and the control tower in the background. That tower was not in Morocco. Rather, renown Hungarian-born director Michael Curtiz (originally Mihaly Kertesz) filmed that scene in front of the Grand Central Airport control tower. Viewing that tower every morning as I approached the KVEA-TV Channel 52 studios somehow added a bit of drama to what Joe and I had going there and the risks we were taking.

But before I started working at KVEA-TV, I had to get KNBC-TV to let me out of my contract, which had just been renewed a few months earlier. I don't think they ever believed my explanation for wanting to leave. They thought for sure I was going back to KABC or perhaps to the CBS network affiliate. I still have a copy of the letter they made me sign stating that I was leaving a major network to devote my career to a managerial position at, what was at that moment, a non-existent television station. The letter included a provision that required me to return and work out the remainder of my contract should the KVEA venture not work out. They really thought I had lost my mind. There were several moments when I actually thought they were right.

While she never voiced it, I'm sure my wife had plenty of doubts as well. She had married a junior high school history teacher, turned college professor, who changed his mind to become a television reporter, who had now decided to become an entrepreneur.

The KVEA venture marked the end of my business relationship with Ed Hookstratten, since there was no real reason to have an agent at that point. A couple of years ago, I talked

KNBC 4

NBC Television Stations Division
National Broadcasting Company, Inc.
3000 West Alameda Avenue
Burbank, CA 91523 818-840-3373

John H. Rohrbeck
Vice President and
General Manager

November 8, 1985

Mr. Frank Cruz
KNBC News
3000 West Alameda Avenue
Burbank, CA 91523

Dear Frank:

This is to confirm that effective today, November 8, 1985, KNBC will honor your request to release you from the personal services agreement between you and KNBC dated January 1, 1985, in order for you to pursue business opportunities at Estrella Communications (KVEA-Channel 52). You have informed us that Estrella Communications has offered you a vice presidency which you will accept.

You agree that for the period through April 1, 1988, the date at which your contractual obligations to KNBC would end under your personal services agreement, you will not work for KCBS-TV and/or KABC-TV in any capacity.

You also agree that if you wish to return to work for a network-owned station, KNBC will have the option and a first refusal right, at our choice, to hire you at your then current contract rate.

On behalf of KNBC, we express our appreciation for everything you have contributed to the station over the years and wish you much success in your new responsibilities.

Sincerely,

John H. Rohrbeck

ACCEPTED AND AGREED:

Frank Cruz

KNBC exit letter – not a vote of confidence

to his son John, an executive at Fox. "I must give your dad credit for what he did for me, I told him."

John replied, "Those Mexican American ties my dad forged rubbed off on me so much so that I'm proud to say my lovely wife is Mexican American."

Back at KVEA, Joe Wallach took the lead as general manager and hired Paul Niedermeyer, from independent station KSFI, as assistant manager. I was vice president of public affairs, which included sales. We carefully positioned the launch of KVEA-TV as presenting additional programming to what KMEX was already offering its loyal Spanish-speaking viewers. Today's marketers would label our approach as creating network effects. In other words, the more people we could expose to Spanish-language television, the more room there would be for programming and accompanying advertising revenues. The Hispanic community, the two stations, the ad agencies and their clients should all benefit.

KMEX General Manager Danny Villanueva's public comments were also supportive of a second Spanish-language station in the region. Due in no small part to this non-competitive approach, his sales revenue increased during our first year on air, as did revenues at the local Spanish-language radio stations.

Hector and Norma Orci were a big part of that growth. The pair of USC graduates had opened their own advertising agency in Los Angeles, intent on helping Spanish-language radio and television stations grow commensurate with their specific market. The small agency was a leader in reaching the Hispanic audiences. The local stations, the advertisers, the audiences, and the Orcis all benefitted.

Of course, it was up to us to introduce the Los Angeles audience to our new station. And, so we did, in a very big way. Joe and I were fortunate to have some real marketing innovators in Carmen Hensch and Giora Briel. This dynamic duo contracted between 250 and 300 billboards in strategic locations in Los Angeles and in Orange County.

Our team and Bishop Mahoney's aide preparing for Spanish-language coverage of Pope John Paul II's visit to Los Angeles

We blanketed Orange County, as well as greater Los Angeles, with billboards because we had been able to install what's called a repeater or translator on Saddleback Mountain, the highest point in Orange County. That device picked up the original signal as it began to fade from our transmitting tower on Mount Wilson in Los Angeles. The repeater then revitalized the signal and sent it south to cover southern Orange

County and all the way down to San Diego. Many television broadcasters relied on these repeaters in the years before cable and satellite television.

Carmen Hensch and Giora Briel devised a three-month billboard marketing campaign that was not only robust with all those signs, but it was uniquely gaining the attention of our future audiences—English and Spanish speaking. So, for the first month, the signage was a single orange ball positioned just to the lower right of the center on a bright blue background. That was it – an orange ball. For the next month, the words "It's Coming" were added above the orange ball. Los Angeles was a buzz . . . "What's coming?" For the last 30 days prior to going on the air, the words, "It's Coming" were replaced with "The LA Channel K-VEA 52 is here." The number 5 was cleverly wrapped around the orange ball.

KVEA billboard

And once that third version of the billboards was installed, we placed KVEA's logo everywhere we legally could—on basketball backboards at city parks, on bus stop benches, etc. Carmen and Giora had even secured a billboard directly across the street from KMEX-TV's headquarters.

One of KVEA Channel 52 basketball backboards

Marketing wasn't our only strategy for success. KVEA's model for friendly competition with KMEX was what Joe called counter programming. For example, if KMEX was airing a *telenovela* (soap opera), we might offer a documentary during the same time slot, providing Spanish-speaking viewers with a choice for the first time. We also added children's programming in the afternoons and aired epic motion pictures that had been dubbed in Spanish. Imagine being able to watch *Dr. Zhivago* or *Mutiny on the Bounty* or *Bambi*, for the first time in your own language, in your own living room.

We're Here and We're Here to Stay – KVEA arrival in Los Angeles poster

The best Spanish language movies and telenovelas in all of Latin America have always been produced in México. And the owners of KMEX also owned Televisa, the largest production studio in México, so the Los Angeles station had its pick of the best. But soap operas don't have a beginning and an end in one sitting, and that can be frustrating to viewers who don't have a regular TV-watching schedule.

Remember, this is well before it was possible to tape programs for later viewing. So what Joe and I did was to create great alternative programing. We went out and bought libraries of great Mexican movies. We got a programmer from México who knew all the Mexican stars and movies. If KMEX was showing telenovelas from 8:00 to 11:00 p.m., we showed a great Mexican movie. Once they aired, all we had to do was let them rest for a few months and then re-broadcast them. In this way, the films were a great investment. Our films featured great stars who were major celebrities of those days. The films that did the best starred México's greatest and most beloved, comedy film star, Cantinflas.

Within six months, we had captured 40 percent of the Spanish television market in Los Angeles. Our advertising sales team, led by Carmen Hensch and Julio Lucero, was selling advertising to both local and national businesses. Carmen and Julio were later joined by Gary McBride who focused on selling time to the large national advertisers. Although the huge Los Angeles market was large enough for two Spanish-language stations, KMEX and KVEA were direct competitors. When we hired away the KMEX top salesman Julio Lucero, it was considered quite a coup. KVEA had attractive pricing and the advertising agencies liked the idea that we were competitive. *Hispanic Business* magazine reported that advertisers spent nearly $60 million in total reaching the Los Angeles-area Spanish-speaking audience in 1985. Nationally, the total was $333.5 million.

As the revenue began to climb, we were able to assemble a great team. We hired announcer Enrique Gratas. He was an Argentinian with a neutral Spanish accent. Joe wanted Enrique to host *VEA Hollywood*, an entertainment/celebrity news show. I disagreed.

"Well what do you want to do?" Joe asked.

My confident response was, "We need news. What KMEX is doing is just repeating news stories from the English-language stations. We need reporters and our own camera crews."

"It's costly," Joe replied.

"Yes, I know," I said. "But the community deserves strong, local news that matters to them."

We immediately hit a home run with the news. We proved to our audience that KVEA-TV was a station that cared about our community and offered coverage of issues pertaining to them.

I relied on the techniques I had learned at KABC-TV and KNBC-TV to mentor young reporters. I went to Félix Gutiérrez, who was by then teaching at USC, and asked if there were any Latino students in his journalism classes who spoke Spanish. I needed a co-anchor and found the wonderful Andrea Kutyas from Uruguay. Her Spanish was perfect. Félix Gutiérrez recommended a great sports reporter in Mario Solis. And then I hired Virginia Jiménez, Miguel Medina, Maria Laria, and Ofelia de la Torre. We produced news, the likes of which KMEX had never done. We were a huge success. The local news programming resulted in skyrocketing advertising sales.

KVEA prime time news team

We also participated in many community activities co-ordinated by Giora Briel and Carmen Hensch. Every year on the 16th of September, Mexican Independence Day, there was a huge parade down Whittier Boulevard in East Los Angeles. The spectator turnout was fantastic, but the production of the event was lacking. The "floats" consisted mainly of some pretty, young women on the back of pick-up trucks. Here was another opportunity for improvement.

I started wondering what happened to all the floats that were used annually in the glorious Pasadena Tournament of Roses Parade. I knew the award-winning float designer Raul Rodríquez, so I drove over to his shop to talk to him. I explained that the September 16th parade is supposed to be something for the community to be proud of. "What would it take to get one of those floats down to East Los Angeles?" I

El rey del Fútbol, the Great Pelé, and me

asked. I shouldn't have been as surprised as I was at his response. Raul, although he was world famous for his artistry, had never forgotten his roots. He gave us the Indonesian entry from the prior year's Rose Parade. That New Year's Day event is always a highlight for Southern Californians, and especially 1986 with its international theme, because the legendary Brazilian soccer player Pelé had served as the grand marshall.

The frame of the "used" float was just perfect for us because it had a high, round top where we could place our logo. KVEA-TV was the hit of the parade in 1986. Rodríquez's generosity changed East Los Angeles' Mexican Independence Day Parade forever. The following year my twins Frankie and Vanessa had a great time riding in the parade right behind the KVEA float.

KVEA's entrant in 1987 East Los Angeles Parade

In 1986 we benefited from a bit of an entrée to Bill Burke who was busy putting together the first Los Angeles Marathon. I had met his wife Congresswoman Yvonne Brathwaite Burke

My twins Vanessa and Frankie in the East Los Angeles Parade

when I was a reporter for KABC-TV. Since she was the first black women in Congress from California, her time and opinions were much sought after. I was lucky enough to interview her in her district office a few times. I approached Bill about the contract to cover the race in Spanish. I explained that running was big in México and Latin America, in fact, I teased him with the prediction that, "one day a Latino is going to win your marathon." KVEA-TV was awarded the contract to cover the race in 1986, and low and behold in 1988 the male and female winners, Martín Mondragón and Blanca Jaime, were both from México.

The other big success was our network-like response and news coverage of events. At the end of 1987, there was a terrible earthquake in El Salvador. Ray Díaz, one of the young reporters who worked in our news department, was from El Salvador. We sent Ray down there to gather footage and fly it back to our Glendale studio. The hope was that we would have fresh footage and not have to rely on network or news agency coverage as KMEX would be doing.

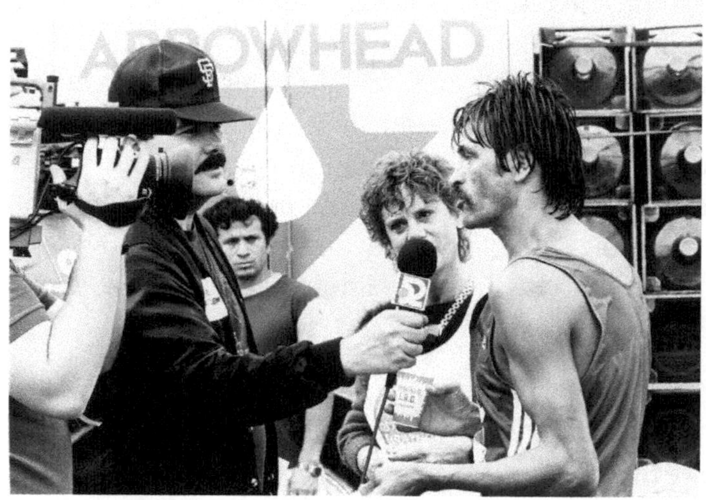

1988 Los Angeles Marathon winner Martin Mondragón

Humberto Luna with crowd at KVEA-sponsored event

At the end of his first day, Ray called me and said he wouldn't be able to leave for another four or five hours because there were so many people at the airport; the departure and arrival gates were swamped. But he could however, get tapes onto Los Angeles-bound flights, even if he couldn't get on himself. Willing passengers and even pilots would pack the aluminum film cans in their carry-on luggage, and we would meet them at the airport with a small cash reward. Ray had the idea to do some man-on-the-street interviews while he waited for a flight for himself. He would approach people and ask, "Do you have any message for your relatives in the United States?" Their replies went something like these:

> "Yes, I just want my aunt and uncle in Los Angeles to know that we are fine and are going to catch the next flight out."
>
> "Yes, the house is damaged, but we are all safe and waiting for you to arrive to help us."
>
> "We are fine, but please send clothing—everything is gone."

The interviews kept on and on. People were so grateful for the opportunity to connect with loved ones. We interrupted the regular programming and ran the interviews without commercials. I asked Joe, "Should we keep going? We're going to need to make up the time with the advertisers."

"Let 'em roll," was Joe's reply.

Our extensive and sensitive coverage of that tragedy was a resounding success, and it won the hearts of the community.

We set up a complete news department with mobile units just like KABC and KNBC. People were stunned by our use of network standards for reporting the news. I hired reporter Bob Navarro as news director. Bob had been with CBS and NBC. Danny Villanueva at KMEX was so concerned about our success that he tried to hire me away from my own station. Indeed, he was able to hire away our sports reporter Mario Solís.

KVEA news van

KVEA Master Control Room

Shortly after Bob came on board, I hired Jaime Jarrín, known today as the Spanish-language "voice of the Dodgers," as our sports director. Jaime had come from Ecuador where he had started a career in broadcasting as a teenager. He came to Los Angeles in 1955, having been hired by radio station KWKW, in Pasadena. The station owner hired Jaime as a news and sports reporter and I would see Jaime at various news conferences, and we would sometimes cover stories together.

Jaime told me a funny story that the owner of KWKW came to him one day and said, "Jaime, we are going to cover Dodger games and you are going to be in the press box." The veteran reporter explained that he didn't know a thing about baseball. Despite his protests, the station owner responded, "Well, you better learn quick because when the season starts, you're going to be our announcer."

So, by the time Jaime joined KVEA, he had announced hundreds of Dodger games. During baseball season Jaime would tape KVEA sports reports early in the afternoon at the station before he drove to Dodger Stadium to cover evening games. And learn the game he did. Jaime Jarrín is now in the Baseball Hall of Fame and is nearing his 60th year broadcasting Los Angeles Dodger games for a Spanish-speaking audience.

The other thing we did was cover the cross-town rivalry—the East LA Classic—the annual football game between Roosevelt and Garfield high schools. I got some pushback on the idea of covering the game because our typical audience was not made up of those who attended the infamous cross-town rivalry—all 25,000 of them. But I explained that their sons and daughters go to the games and that we could begin to cultivate a younger audience.

We got a professional camera crew to cover the annual match up played at the beautiful East Los Angeles College stadium, now called the Weingart Stadium. It was the first time ever that an eastside sports event was shown live on television. I remember that night so well. Once I saw that the crew was set up and ready, I left and stopped at a friend's bar on Beverly and Atlantic boulevards; I knew the crowd at Ricky's would be watching the game. It was quite a personal thrill to witness their excitement.

Our ability to professionally cover the iconic cross-town rivalry began in 1985 when I had won a contract to cover the Los Angeles Raiders in Spanish, which had never been done before. My entrepreneurial spirit was flying high. The contract was for the four preseason games that were not under contract with one of the major networks. I needed to put together a crew so that we could take the big engineering truck down to the Los Angeles Coliseum to cover the games. We needed to hire a producer and technical folks. I had an interview with a man who was a broadcast engineer who had recently moved from the East Coast, "I'll do the Raiders for you since I'm now living here with my family."

So, I signed him up just before a Raiders' game coming up that weekend.

Now that we had a crew and a producer, my assistant Margie Medina reminded me about the idea to cover the Roosevelt and Garfield high school game. I asked the producer if he would be interested in a high school game between two big town rivals.

"Nah, I'm not interested," he said and that concluded our meeting.

Fast forward about an hour, and my office phone rings and Margie informed me, "Mr. Cruz, that producer is on the phone, again." I picked up the receiver and he blurted out, "You know that high school game? Well, I was sitting down with my wife and it turns out she went to Garfield High School and she looked me straight in the eyes and said, 'You go do that game!'"

What we were able to do the first six months after launching KVEA in November 1985 was absolutely fantastic. We've since celebrated several reunions of that start-up group. You ought to see the passion, the enthusiasm that comes out of those parties. We all experienced a sense of belonging to the team and to a shared mission to build a Spanish-language station that was first class. We accomplished that for ourselves and for the community and for our investors. I'm still amazed that 30 years later some of the team still join the annual party from across the county.

VOLUME 1, NUMBER 1 Estrella Communications, Inc. Newsletter December 1, 1985

EN EL AIRE

VEA 52

KVEA-52 OPENS A NEW ERA

On November 24, 1985 a new era in the world of Spanish-language communications starts in Los Angeles as KVEA-52 debuts its innovative programming over the airwaves of our city.

"We believe our first day on the air will cause some excitement and attract attention," says Joseph Wallach, who serves as President and Chief Operating Officer of KVEA-52. "This will provide the audience with a taste of things to come."

Estrella Communications Inc., KVEA-52's parent company, has assembled a staff of highly experienced professionals who have strong ties with Southern California's sizable Latino Community.

"I plan to utilize my contacts and expertise at the network level in my new position," explains Frank Cruz, Vice President in charge of Community Affairs. Cruz joins KVEA-52 after working 14 years in journalism at KNBC as well as KABC. "The potential of Spanish-language television is incredible. It's an honor to be a part of its development."

Proclaimed "El Canal de Los Angeles" (The Channel of Los Angeles), KVEA-52 is the first full-service, local independent Latino-targeted TV station in Los Angeles. Its debut points to the growing strength and financial influence of Los Angeles' 3.4 million Spanish-speaking people.

"We will reach Latinos throughout Southern California," adds Wallach, who was director of Globo-TV in Brazil. "The strategic position of our antenna, on Mount Wilson, enables us to cover the entire metropolitan area. Including Los Angeles, Riverside, Orange, Kern and San Bernardino."

"For a long time Latinos in Los Angeles did not enjoy the advantages of an alternative to the Spanish-language programming they had to watch," comments Armando Corral, director of sales. KVEA-52 fills the needs of the community. One of my biggest satisfactions has been the support given to the station by the smaller businesses of the community and KVEA-52 has it from the beginning."

Now with KVEA-52 on the air, the Spanish-language television business in Los Angeles is changed for the good. The new station's debut marks a new era in the competitive world of communications.

JOE WALLACH
President and
Chief Operating Officer.

Sample of Telemundo publicity

Carmen Hensch, our unofficial historian, has coordinated these reunions. In July 2008, we pulled off a surprise party for Joe Wallach at the Castaway Restaurant high in the hills above Burbank. We told his wife to just say she was taking him out to dinner for his birthday. All of us got there first and very early. He just couldn't believe it. Writers, camera crew members, reporters—they are still around and really care about what we had done at KVEA-TV.

I later emceed another reunion and shared how great it was to be part of what we had accomplished. "You have since moved on in your careers," I said. "But you were all equal participants in this creation."

A few articles have been written over the years about what we did at KVEA, but I'm the first person to really document what we accomplished. After all, I did have a front row seat in its development.

What began to happen was, that while KVEA and KMEX were in competition on the West Coast at the end of 1985 and into the spring of 1986, our advertising sales and audience ratings were so impressive that the Reliance people were beginning to envision the possibility of developing a nationwide network, because in the background of our success was a very serious case winding its way through the courts. The outcome would impact what was then called the Spanish International Network (SIN). That court case threatened

KVEA interviews me at station anniversary party

KMEX and other SIN U.S. television stations owned and controlled by the Azcárraga family in México.

What if they disappeared? What if the court forced them into bankruptcy or forced a sale of SIN?

Those questions, coupled with the meteoric and dazzling success of KVEA, led to some serious discussions about starting a new Spanish-language television network in the United States.

Chapter Eight

How Long Would It Take to Assemble Our Own Network?

Our talks with the Reliance people centered around four major points: the financial and ratings success of KVEA-TV, the explosive Hispanic demographic data emanating from the 1980 census, the meteoric rise of Latinos in American popular culture and the arts, and an opportunity posed by the legal case jeopardizing the Azcárraga family. That family owned the U.S. television network SIN and the station ownership group Spanish International Communications Corp. (SICC). Azcárraga owned almost all of the network, but officially only 20 percent of the station group, in order to conform to FCC rules regarding foreign ownership. He controlled the station group through "*presta nombres*"- owners who either worked for him or who were business associates of his.

The demographic studies that were coming out of the 1980 census were startling. "If the numbers are that high, and if we could only get our share of the advertising revenue, hell, this would be an enormous success," Reliance Chairman Saul Steinberg would say. The numbers were what drove investors; increasing advertising revenue follow population growth.

The emerging business ramifications of the immigration numbers that were being released slowly from the 1980 census were a main ingredient in an intoxicating brew. In popular media, we would read story after story about the numbers of Hispanics and the growth of that population. We anticipated that the big advertisers like General Motors, Ford, Pepsi, and Proctor & Gamble were looking at the same numbers. Even Coors posted billboards touting, "Coors, the Beer for the Decade of the Hispanic." Income levels were rising, and the potential buying power of this emerging domestic market fueled many future discussions with Reliance Capital.

A staggering 62 percent growth of the Hispanic population between 1970 and 1980 begged a response from corporate America. Twenty million strong by the 1980s, Hispanics were forecast to soon reach full participation in "the American dream." Nearing the end of what the media had labelled the "Decade of the Hispanic," the Cuban American Council reported that, between 1980 and 1988, "Hispanics experienced a 34 percent growth rate, compared with an 8 percent rate in the general population." The increase was due to a steady flow of Hispanic immigrants and higher than general population birth rates.

Thus, the young age of the Hispanic market was also a factor that was attractive to advisors. Young families needed more diapers, more laundry soap, more breakfast cereal, etc. etc. Hispanics represented more than 30 percent of total

U.S. immigration and birth rates, which were more than 20 per thousand, compared with 16 per thousand for the general population.

Political consultant Arnoldo S. Torres reported in 1985 that the median age of the U.S. Hispanic population was 22. Reaching this young audience would be less complicated than others because more than half of the Hispanic population lived in either California or Texas. If New York, Illinois, Florida, New México, Arizona, Colorado, and New Jersey were included, an advertising campaign could reach 90 percent of Hispanics. With the rapid increase of young consumers, the U.S. Hispanic consumer market had reached $171 billion. Demand for basic domestic goods for young families promoted the evolution of a national Hispanic market in the eyes of Madison Avenue advertising agencies seeking Spanish speaking viewers.

I recall comforting my compadres and visiting students at CCNMA meetings in the 1970s and 1980s, "Time and numbers are on our side."

Popular culture was another ingredient in what was looking like a mixture that could delight. The Reliance people would say things like, "My gosh, we're seeing a cultural shift play out here." They were right. In addition to the economic factors was the increased representation of Latinos in popular culture.

In music, we witnessed the crossover popularity of comedian and writer Richard Anthony "Cheech" Marin, former East L.A. garage band Los Lobos. Carlos Santana's music could be heard everywhere, Tucson's Linda Ronstadt began to record in Spanish, and Richie Valens' memory was revived on the radio coinciding with the popular release of the theatrical motion picture, *La Bamba*. Television and movies were also producing such major stars as Jimmy Smits in *LA*

Law and Edward James Olmos in *Miami Vice* in addition to his award-winning performances in the motion pictures *Zoot Suit* and *Stand and Deliver*.

These successes heralded later projects like Robert Redford's direction of Ruben Blades and Sonia Braga in the critically acclaimed, *Milagro Beanfield War* and public television's *American Family*.

In the world of sports, Los Angeles rallied around the sensation of Dodger pitcher Fernando Valenzuela and Tom Flores coaching the Los Angeles Raiders and their quarterback Jim Plunkett to a Super Bowl victory in 1983.

In the literary world, the works of Latino authors like Nobel Prize winner Miguel Angel Asturias and Isabel Allende established Latin American literature's contribution to United States' culture.

KVEA's success, the exploding demographics, and Latino penetration into popular culture were the certain and quantifiable elements. The unknown factor that remained was the degree of legal sanctions that would be levied against Spanish International Communications Corp. The television station group was comprised of KMEX in Los Angeles, KFTV in Fresno, WLTV in Miami, WXTV in New Jersey, KWEX in San Antonio, KDTV in San Francisco, and KTVW in Phoenix. The Federal Communications Commission (FCC) was examining the ownership relationship between these TV stations and Mexican, media baron Emilio Azcárraga and his family.

Further obscuring proprietorship of the Spanish International Communications Corp. (SICC) was the Azcárraga-owned and controlled Spanish International Network (SIN). With names so similar perhaps to confuse, SIN supplied programming to, and sold advertising time on the SICC-owned stations. On that basis, in January 1986, FCC Administrative Law Judge John H. Conlin denied the renewal of all broadcast licenses of the SICC television stations. His conclusion was that SICC was "illegally controlled and influenced" by the Mexican television magnate Azcárraga.

According to the *Los Angeles Times*, the Azcárraga family had made loans to hand-picked employees and business associates, who were American citizens, who then purchased ownership in the U.S.-licensed stations. This generally made the stations dependent on the Mexican Azcárraga family and thus exceeded the 20 percent maximum foreign ownership law for stations.

The case against SICC was complex with appeal after appeal that only served to prolong the inevitable. We knew the whole organization was in violation, but no one knew what the ultimate outcome would be. The effect of the appeal court's decision could be devastating to SICC and SIN, and a huge opportunity for anyone who could step in and provide Spanish-language programming in its place, i.e. a replacement coast-to-coast network.

The Reliance people were drunk with what was happening at KVEA and the growing demographics, "This market is massive!" they said. "The average age and the numbers of children—it's such a growing audience." Collectively, all the motivating ingredients were becoming an irresistible concoction. Just one question remained: How could we position ourselves to take advantage of any prohibition levied against the Azcárraga family?

All the excited phone calls and discussions culminated in a May 1986 meeting at the Reliance building in midtown Manhattan. Sitting around a huge table, the Reliance people kicked off the meeting saying, "We hear that the appeals could go against them [SICC]. What do we need to do to be prepared for whatever the outcome is?"

They were envisioning a void and wanting a contingency plan to address a possible rare opportunity. I remember Joe Wallach and I sort of leading the discussion from that point.

> We responded, "The prudent strategy would be to approach independent stations in Hispanic markets, such as San Antonio, Tucson, El Paso, San Diego, etc. and make attractive offers to buy airtime from 6:00 to 8:00 p.m. for Spanish-language programming." Such block time purchases were used to launch Spanish-language radio programming in the 1920s and 1930s. "If all goes well," we added, "we could expand from 6:00 to 10:00 p.m., which is what FOX did to start its network."

That first idea was to assemble a Spanish-language television network on a piecemeal basis. Joe and I explained that we could go to the key Hispanic markets and identify struggling independent stations (not affiliated with the major networks ABC, CBS, or NBC) in Denver, Houston, Miami, and a couple of California cities. Because these stations could not compete with prime-time network programs, we figured they might be willing to sell evening time which we would use to offer programming counter to the English-language networks in these key Hispanic markets.

We explained that the programming would come from KVEA. These indie stations would surely be attracted to the same numbers we were providing to Reliance, because sharing advertising revenue would be an important part of the arrangement. Depending on the size of the market, we would propose paying a flat fee for the time or a percentage of the advertising revenue or a combination. In the bigger markets we would give a fee plus a share of the sponsorship advertising revenue.

The process of sharing the KVEA programming that was dubbed "bicycling" by SIN in the 1960s and early 1970s, because the film or videotape was literally placed in a can and, in some cases, driven to affiliate stations. This would have been dated material, such as the Mexican-made and Spanish-dubbed films that were so successful for us at KVEA.

Reliance CEO Henry Silverman and Chairman Saul Steinberg looked at us in protest saying, "But that would take a lot of time. It's too slow and would take a lot of work and a lot of time."

The non-starter for this incremental approach was that it wouldn't provide the flexibility we needed to have should the appeals go against the Azcárragas. "What's the alternative?" they asked.

"You buy stations," we explained, "You buy stations in key Hispanic markets. It still takes time and it's costly, but it could be much quicker than buying block times and bicycling approach."

The decision was that we would expand by buying stations. All agreed it was the best approach.

So, it was back to Drexel Burnham Lambert and Michael Milken. This time it was to ask for ten times their first investment. At that same time, we learned that an underachieving entity—like KVEA had been—was being offered for sale. The John Blair Entertainment Company owned radio and television stations, a publishing house, and a direct mail operation. *True Confessions* and *Modern Romance* magazines were also theirs. The decision to buy John Blair came quick, and

Saul Steinberg's aggressive business approach came through. In September 1986, the John Blair Company gave us a platform on which to build the second coast-to-coast, Spanish-language television network.

John Blair had been a problematic company with financial issues. We paid $333 million for the eight radio stations, the four television stations, the publishing division, and the direct mail business. Henry Silverman immediately spun off the radio stations and recouped the initial investment, and then some. We sold two television stations that were not located in strategic Hispanic markets, and we kept WSCV in Miami and WKAQ Channel 2 in Puerto Rico with its large production facility.

Channel 2 was the most popular station in Puerto Rico. Much of the island's population of about 9 million is bilingual—English and Spanish. From our brief, but thorough, due diligence work prior to the purchase, we knew that the Blair Company package contained that station in Puerto Rico. Channel 2 had a reputation for producing good content in English and Spanish. We also learned that many huge U.S. companies test marketed their products and television commercials in Puerto Rico. The successful products and commercials would be distributed and aired throughout Latin America. We believed the same approach could also be used for the U.S. Hispanic market.

Our television network then consisted of stations in Miami, Puerto Rico, and Los Angeles. We wasted no time making additional key acquisitions with the proceeds from the sale of the radio stations. In October 1986, we purchased WNJU in New Jersey/New York for $75 million and a month later KSTS in San Francisco for $13.5 million, concluding with WSNS in Chicago. That last purchase was a real coup as we basically bought the station out from under SICC. We then had critical mass in the six major Hispanic markets coast to coast and Puerto Rico. We were ready to launch at any moment; we just needed to brand our network. We needed a name.

We had several discussions on the topic, by phone, at meetings at KVEA, and when Joe and I would fly back to New York. Basically, each meeting started off with the same question: "Now we've got it, what shall we call it?"

The production studios in Puerto Rico were called Telemundo. We tossed around "globo" this and that, but it all seemed too close to Globo Brazil that Joe had assembled. I said, "Hey, Telemundo is a good name and it's known. Let's just keep it alive." The built-in equity of the name Telemundo won the day. Telemundo went live in five major U.S. metropolitan areas and Puerto Rico in January 1987, just five months after the Blair acquisition.

"Hey, Telemundo is a good name and it's known. Let's just keep it alive."

What we did next was establish what are called affiliate agreements, based off our five U.S.-owned and operated stations on the mainland. In the broadcasting world those are known as O&Os. It should be explained that WKAQ in Puerto Rico served a quite separate market and we used the station with a formula customized to our needs and their market. They produced their own programming at WKAQ and we continued to use the island as a laboratory, of sorts, for soapies. By running the telenovelas on WKAQ first, we could test whether or not the productions could "have legs" in Latin American markets and the accompanying advertising revenue.

Having many affiliate stations is a key ingredient to selling advertising time to the agencies on Madison Avenue. If you can make a block sale, you can offer better pricing making your outlets more attractive.

Gary McBride was the man who could make those block sales happen. Gary had gone to Thunderbird for an international business degree before working in Latin America. He would complain some about having to "explain to Gringos" that the Spanish-language television stations were a refuge for Latinos in the U.S. Gary pursued new and daring strategies with Madison Avenue advertisers which allowed us to complete for those sales. In addition to advertising time, the big nationals like Colgate-Palmolive and Pepsi, wanted us to organize large community events that they could sponsor. He established cooperative relationships with major entities like MTV and Pepsi, which were Telemundo's entre to the music industry by assisting with hiring Gloria Esteban for a Pepsi commercial we aired.

Again, to make our block sales ever more attractive, we worked on signing up those affiliate station arrangements in person. Joe and I were travelling all around the country to Dallas, Brownsville, Tucson, Albuquerque, El Paso, San Antonio, and more. We would approach these independent station owners with the opportunity to maintain control, of course, but become affiliated with Telemundo, carry our programming, and share the advertising revenue. I can't tell you how hectic 1986 and 1987 were, flying back and forth across the country. Joe would conduct some of the meetings and I handled others.

Eventually, we completed contracts with many station owners by telephone. Honestly, they were sort of glad to hear from us. Many of these affiliates were the indie stations from which we would have otherwise purchased programming time had we gone the slow route to forming the network. They couldn't compete with the networks in prime time, but as an affiliate of Telemundo they could offer counter programming with our quality Spanish-language content for the Hispanic population in their markets.

Glimpse of Joe Wallach's engaging personality

In some areas like in Salinas, Sacramento, and Phoenix, we also approached owners of low-power UHF stations in order to further penetrate the Spanish-language market.

Then it was back to Drexel Burnham Lambert and Michael Milken because we used the money from the John Blair spinoffs very quickly. By that time, Paul Neidermeyer had left Los Angeles to run our San Francisco station and I was running KVEA. What the investors were counting on was the demographic data being attractive enough to advertising America to buy air time with us. It became apparent that this was going to be a rougher go than any of us anticipated. The problem in approaching Madison Avenue was that the agencies didn't respond quickly to the population data. Their advertising purchases were based on the Nielsen and Arbitron audience ratings. We were a brand-new network and our audience didn't have rating agencies' diaries and recorders installed in their homes. Because of that lack of customary data, the ad agencies didn't have any metrics with which to establish pricing for an emerging audience.

Meanwhile, the courts forced the sale of SICC to the U.S. holding entity—Hallmark. In 1988 Hallmark and First Capital became the owners and renamed the network Univision. The Azcárragas had been able to sell SICC as an entity; they didn't have to break it up. This was not an outcome we had anticipated. Hallmark paid $301.5 million for the station ownership group.

So that meant there were now two Spanish-language networks trying to sell advertising time to Madison Avenue. The primary objectives of these agencies were the big sporting events that were always a safe bet even if there was a downturn in the economy. Therefore, our programming was not high on their radar. Additionally, the advertisers were anxious about the newness of the market and this new competition between Hallmark/Univision and Telemundo. But the most serious push back from the ad agencies was that they didn't have the metrics.

"How do we measure reach and frequency on your stations?" they asked. "We're just banking on your word!"

In many ways, we were ahead of the curve. Advertising America on Madison Avenue still saw us as a market yet to be proven; the rating agencies didn't really measure Hispanic households until the 1990s, and still don't, many say. In the late 1980s, it would have been great if we could have sold content to the cable companies, like producers can today. But in those days, you had to pay cable companies like Cox, Charter, and Falcon to carry your content.

The country also experienced a downturn in the economy in 1988-89. This combined with the absence of metrics from diaries and recorders in homes, as well as advertisers fixated on the big sporting events, we were struggling. As the newcomer, we were the first to be cut off, and Univision would get the lion's share of the national advertising revenues.

In light of the general economy rocked by the savings and loan crisis, the tough competition for advertising income, and a capable competitor we hadn't planned on, our next decision demonstrated our shared entrepreneur spirit.

Even after the sale to Hallmark, a majority of Univision's programming came from Televisa's production studios in México. That was another outcome that we had not anticipated. We had a choice. We could have continued our strategy of counter programming against Televisa's excellent and cheaper Mexican content, or we could develop domestic programming. We started with the news.

We leveraged the relationship between our financier Michael Milken and his good friend and client Ted Turner. Turner was interested in news all over the world. Soon CNN/Telemundo News had access to Turner's vast news-gathering organization. We were able to combine the work of their camera crews in México, and Central and South America with our on-air reporters in Miami and put together a state-of-the-art newscast.

Our news directors would just download the feed from CNN, and the reporter would begin, "In Nicaragua this afternoon, there were protests . . ." We'd use CNN footage from Nicaragua to enhance our reporting. By then, due to the wonders of satellites, we could download the footage and then search through the stories we were interested in. In those days, our station in Miami had all our equipment for the news broadcasts. The staff would spend the whole day putting together the half-hour evening newscast. SIN had nowhere near the quality we were able to achieve at Telemundo because of the agreement reached between Reliance and CNN. Similarly, we were able to put together another locally produced show. Telemundo/MTV became a popular show starring Latino music groups.

About then, I had this crazy idea. I could see that the Univision stations had their beautifully produced telenovelas, but all the settings, especially the outdoor settings, were videotaped entirely in México. I thought, why don't we come up with a U.S. telenovela or "soapie." We could get one of the best writers and film in U.S. locations that were familiar to our Hispanic audiences. So, we did. In 1988 *Angelica, Mi Vida* was the first telenovela produced in the United States.

One episode was about a Cuban family in Miami, another focused on a Puerto Rican family in New York, and another followed a Mexican family in Los Angeles in 1988. It was a tricky formula because of the cost. One episode could cost five or six times more to shoot in the United States than it did in México. We hired the most important telenovela writer, Cuban-born Delia Fiallo. She would go on to teach her writing formula to writers all over the world as she is considered one of the most distinguished romance novel writers. With Delia's amazing plots, we attempted to counter the, by then, tried and proven formula of Univision having the pick of the best of the less-expensive, Televisa-produced telenovelas to be aired in the U.S.

Our telenovelas had a good run. Unlike English-language soap operas in the U.S. that can literally endure for decades (think *All My Children*), Spanish-language telenovelas have a definite beginning and an end. The formula is about 140 to 160 chapters airing nightly in the 6 to 8 p.m. time slot, after the 5 p.m. news broadcast. Procter and Gamble even utilized advertising called product placement, which was quite new at the time, by adding some of their products as props on the set. Some of our stars—like Gloria Torres Hayes—also did some commercials for them. Then we produced another U.S.-based program called *Cita con el Amor* that was similar to *The Dating Game*.

But the program that was extremely successful was *Cara a Cara*, with host María Laria. We shot it at 6:00 in the evenings in Los Angeles, and it was aired in the late evenings on the East Coast. The crew would come in and rearrange the news room stage and María Laria would welcome her guests. The late-night hit ran the gamut of controversial topics and celebrity interviews; it was a regular Ellen DeGeneres- and Oprah Winfrey-style show. We produced it at KVEA in late 1988. María Laria is a Cuban American who came to the States as a very young girl and went to school in Boston. At KVEA, she was co-anchoring the news with Enrique Gratas; they were a great team. I think María may have come to us with the idea for a talk show. *Cara a Cara* went into national syndication via satellite. Its success prompted Univision to copy the show with their host Cristina Saralegui.

The difficulty was that we had begun to incur debt because of our expansion with affiliate agreements, low-power station acquisitions, and domestic productions. And our operating budget was tough when compared to Univision's with its access to low-cost programs from México. The big problem that began to emerge was the amount of money that we had borrowed from Milken and the advertising revenue that was not coming in as rapidly as we thought it would. The five O&Os had their own local and national sales force. What we would sell were the national programs. We could go to the big agencies and offer them exposure on all the five O&Os and our many affiliates, with good results, but increasingly not good enough to satisfy our investors.

Venture capitalists want to see some positive results in two or three years after their investment. My plea had been to give us more time. They could see the growth of the market, but it just wasn't translating into revenue growth fast enough. I was trying to make Telemundo resemble U.S. television networks like NBC, ABC, and CBS, but I was running out of time and investor patience.

Several advertising agencies were popping up then as well. The successful agency in Los Angeles was Orci. The husband-and-wife team's company grew as a result of the growth of Univision and Telemundo. What USC grads Hector and Norma Orci were trying to do was to get advertising money from Madison Avenue; they were really the spokespersons for the growing Hispanic numbers and they developed their own versions of metrics and ratings.

It is interesting to note that in 2017, the *Los Angeles Times* did a big story, just after Donald Trump's inauguration, about how the Orcis began their agency. In the interview, the couple voiced concerns about anti-immigrant rhetoric and the effects it might have on the populations of people who already feel ignored by the major networks.

Another unanticipated challenge we encountered was a lot of opposition from Latino activists to the sale of SICC to Hallmark and the financing of Telemundo by Reliance. Many groups were concerned that non-Hispanics owned both Spanish-language networks. Efforts had been made to block the sale of Univision, and a lot of heated debates centered around exploitation of the Hispanic community. Victor Valle wrote about it in the *Los Angeles Times* and so did Félix Gutiérrez for the Associated Press. It was something I had to balance out in my own mind. I used to say, "At least we're putting on some good, relevant stories." But, whenever I'd go to an event and make a speech, I would experience some level of push back. To me it was a strategic decision. I used to liken the situation to teaching. I couldn't have taught at Long Beach State if the entities weren't there to form the infrastructure. But I've got to say, the backlash was hurtful.

Joe left KVEA and Telemundo in early 1988. In his case, Joe had wanted to run the network, and Silverman and others agreed only if he would have moved to New York. Joe didn't want to live in New York. While this disagreement was going on, the Reliance people were constantly visiting, and invariably the talks would come down to finances. I was then in charge of the operation out here on the West Coast. It did seem that their oversight had been preying on Joe, and it wasn't that much fun for me either.

Henry Silverman would stay at the Ritz Carlton hotel in Laguna Niguel when he came to the Los Angeles area. That was not far from my house, so we spent a lot of time in the car driving into town together and discussing Telemundo and how to get advertising America to buy more time from us.

Reliance Chief Operating Officer Don Raider, a big burley former Marine, would visit all the time too, sometimes with Henry, but often on his own. Don would get straight to the point, "Now let's talk about the advertising revenues . . ."

On October 1, 1987, Don had flown out and was staying at the Bonaventure Hotel in downtown Los Angeles. That morning, I was driving to our Glendale studio. Headed north on the 605 Freeway, my car started to swerve pretty badly. I pulled over only to find many other drivers standing outside their cars parked in the shoulder. They were all looking at their tires. Our tires weren't flat—we had experienced an earthquake. I called my assistant, Margie Medina, on my two-way radio. She was glad to hear from me because Don had called to cancel our scheduled meeting at KVEA that morning.

I called the Bonaventure and was connected to Don's room. "Frank I'm leaving," he said. "I'm getting in a cab right now."

"Oh, Don," I said, "really it's no problem. I'll be there in a few minutes, and if you must leave, I'll drive you to the airport."

"Frank, I'm leaving now," he repeated and hung up the phone.

I later learned that the laundry room for hotel operations was located directly above Don's room. When the earthquake struck, one of the large commercial washing machines came loose from its mooring and shot right out the side of the building. All the exterior walls of the Bonaventure are glass. As the tall hotel swayed back and forth with the earthquake, Don watched that washing machine fly past his window and down to the ground far below. Don took a cab to the airport. I don't think I ever did see him again in Los Angeles.

With Joe gone, I could see the writing on the wall. Our dream had turned into a numbers game. Considering the consequences of leaving Telemundo had begun to occupy a lot of my time; I had always thought of myself as one who never stepped away from a challenge. But, looking back over my career, I realize that if I had been having fun and feeling like I was pursuing my passion to educate and working to illuminate the Latino experience, no challenge had been too great.

But my last days at the network had been consumed with justifying numbers to financial types who had no connection to the reasons Joe and I had purchased our first station, KVEA-TV, in the first place—to offer the Latino community relevant programming and quality news broadcasts. I was really struggling with an internal values conflict. Ultimately, with my life's purpose sidelined in favor of producing the right numbers for venture capitalists, I made a choice that I hope I would make again, if I had the chance to relive those days. I left Telemundo in 1990.

Soon afterward, Reliance Capital sold the network to Sony, which sold it to Leon Black and Bastion Capital, which sold it to NBC in 2001. Then NBC merged with Vivaldi in 2004 and became NBC Universal, which was purchased over time by Comcast from 2009 to 2013 for a total cost of over $30 billion. Joe and I always knew what we had created; each succeeding acquisition of Telemundo reinforced what our instincts had told us back in 1986.

Henry Silverman went on to head up Days Inn, then AVIS/Budget car rental, then the Cendant Corporation. Now he is senior advisor and vice chairman at Guggenheim Partners.

Many years later, I received a call from Marta Tapias-Mansfield who asked me to join her for lunch with Steve Clarkston, the general manager of KNBC-TV in Los Angeles.

I'd known Marta for years in sales and public relations at Telemundo. At lunch, Marta pointed to me and said to Steve, "You know, Telemundo wouldn't be here if it weren't for this man sitting right here."

"What are you talking about?" he asked. The lunch was sometime in 2011, and Telemundo had been recently purchased by NBC.

Imagine, the company that made me sign a letter promising that I would return to complete my contract if KVEA-TV did not work out, had purchased Telemundo for nearly two billion dollars. From Steve's reaction, it dawned on me that NBC didn't know anything about the origins of Telemundo.

I enjoyed recreating the whole story for Steve. His jaw dropped. The popular misconception around NBC had been that it was the Puerto Rico station that had created the Telemundo network. Indeed, that's the way Telemundo tells the story—an urban legend reinforced by the network itself. I was proud to set the record straight at that luncheon, and here in my memoir.

Joe Wallach, Carmen Hensch and me at Joe's birthday party and KVEA/Telemundo reunion

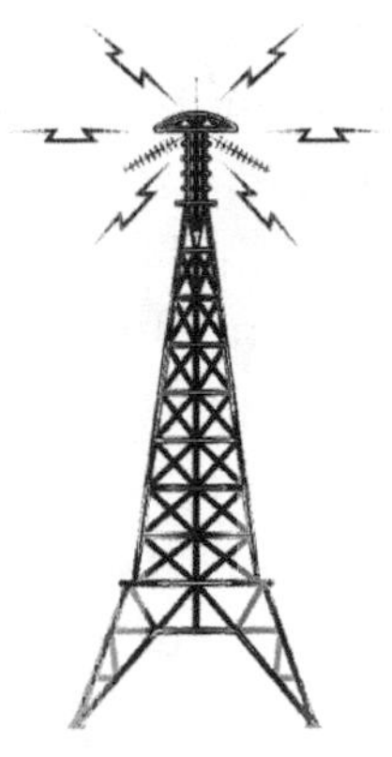

Chapter Nine

Mr. Cruz, It's the White House Calling, Again

Now, did I have any regrets about leaving Telemundo? Do all tough decisions have consequences? Absolutely. I missed the day-to-day contact with the many talented people Joe and I had hired at the network. Conversely, I know I would not have wanted to go through the series of staff buyouts that plagued the network for many years. But I must also admit that when it was announced in 2001 that NBC had purchased Telemundo Communications Group Inc. from Sony Pictures Entertainment and a consortium of investors for $1.98 billion, I felt not just a small twinge of regret. With that purchase, NBC became the only traditional broadcast network with a business fully devoted to developing and airing programming specifically created for the Spanish-speaking market. I would have liked to have been a part of that.

The irony of NBC's purchase of Telemundo was the source of much sick humor among my family and close friends.

We recalled my exit interview from KNBC-TV in 1985, when the station management had made me sign a non-compete letter, wherein I promised that I would rejoin the local Los Angeles station and work out the balance of my contract if, and when my new venture at KVEA-TV failed. Either they hadn't believed my KVEA story or had believed it would fail. Either way they didn't want me to land at a competitor station. Yet, there they were paying nearly $2 billion for the result of what Joe and I had started at KVEA!

The Power of Personal Community Building: No One "Makes It" on Their Own

I used the time after Telemundo to enjoy family life and renew old friendships. At the same time, I had been bitten hard by the entrepreneurial bug and was exploring new business opportunities. Manny Sánchez and I had met back at East Los Angeles College and had become friends. By 1990, he was recognized as a rising star in the Los Angeles Latino community. He had earned a law degree, and at the time we reconnected, he was chief operating officer of healthcare giant Blue Cross. That was quite an amazing ascension from the barrio. He was a brilliant guy and obviously had an in-depth understanding of the insurance business.

Manny proposed the idea that he and I start the first Latino-owned life insurance company. He knew of a licensed shell company in Austin, Texas, that insurance giant Nationwide was interested in selling. Not long after that initial conversation, Manny and I purchased Gulf Atlantic Life. We moved the headquarters, with all the associated licenses to California and were soon able to form a partnership with insurance giant TransAmerica and set up offices in their downtown Los Angeles high-rise at 12th and Olive Streets.

My first big sale made us the life insurance provider for all of California State University system faculty and staff (tens of thousands).

Manny and I understood the power of relationship building, locally and nationally. One example of how we integrated the company into the national scene began in 1991 when California had sustained a couple of economic snubs from Washington, D.C. There had been a big program to study earthquakes, which from a purely practical point of view should have been awarded to Cal Tech or one of our renown state research universities. The program was instead granted to the State University of New York at Buffalo. Shortly thereafter, a company based in Texas was awarded the contract to build a linear particle accelerator in the United States.

In response to these disappointments, a bipartisan group of California legislators got together, under the then leadership of Governor Pete Wilson and U.S. Senator Alan Cranston. They formed the California Institute for Federal Policy Research. The collaborative group basically proclaimed: "Yes, we're Democrats and Republicans, but we now have to come together to fight for the economic prosperity of the state that we represent and love." I'm proud to say that Gulf Atlantic Life was one of the first sponsoring companies.

At institute meetings, I had the chance to meet the likes of Leon Panetta and Don Edwards from the political world as well as a host of representatives from great companies and educational institutions that were committed to California's prosperity. A California Republican turned Democrat, Panetta served our nation in several high-level leadership roles, ranging from White House chief of staff to director of the CIA. Don Edwards represented Californians in Congress for 32 years and served as chairman of the House Subcommittee on Civil

Liberties and Civil Rights for 23 years. I was honored to serve as chair of the institute's executive board for a term.

32-year U.S. Congressman from California Don Edwards and me at California Institute for Federal Policy Research

A couple of years into what was to be a four-year partnership with Manny, I sat in my beautiful corner office in the TransAmerica high rise in downtown and watched South Los Angeles on fire. It was the spring of 1992, and the city had erupted in outrage in response to the not-guilty verdicts against four Los Angeles police officers who were caught on video savagely beating and kicking an unarmed African American truck driver. During the ensuing Los Angeles riots, more than 100 fires were set, protestors blocked freeway traffic, dozens of people were killed, and thousands were wounded in encounters with police and National Guard troops that President George H. Bush had ordered to the scene.

Watching from that 12th-floor window was like being in a news helicopter but without the assignment or tools to help people understand what was really going on. My town was on fire and I felt helpless. My work with the institute seemed somehow irrelevant as flames engulfed the state's largest city.

Gulf Atlantic Downtown Los Angeles office with a view of USC

A few months earlier, I had run into attorney Mickey Kantor at a luncheon at the California Club in downtown Los Angeles. Because he was an expert on the changing demographics of California and the nation, I had interviewed him for my Emmy-winning KNBC-TV special, *The Latinization of Los Angeles*. As we waited to be seated at the luncheon, Mickey asked me who I was planning to vote for in the upcoming presidential primary. I explained that with so many vying for the Democratic nod, I hadn't yet made up my mind. "Who are you voting for?" I asked. He quickly responded, "Bill Clinton." I hadn't heard of Clinton, so after that luncheon I began to research his qualifications.

I was glad to have read something about Clinton when I got a phone call from Mickey who announced that he was heading up the Clinton for President campaign, and he had an opportunity for me to support the candidate. We both knew a weakness of the Clinton candidacy was that he hadn't had any business experience and no real ties to corporate America. To demonstrate Clinton's ability to engage the business community, Mickey explained that he was putting together two groups of executives—50 on the East Coast and 50 on the West Coast—who would participate in a simulcast endorsement of Bill Clinton for president. I liked what I had read about Clinton and agreed to participate.

In mid-December 1992, then President-elect Clinton convened a summit of business leaders to Arkansas from a wide variety of industries to inform him on the challenges and opportunities in the various business sectors of the U.S. economy. I was honored to participate as a minority business owner. I responded to Clinton's interest in the challenges that small businesses encountered that impeded our growth. At that December 1992 Little Rock Economic Summit, I had the pleasure of meeting a lot of heavy hitters, such as Texas politician and businessman Henry Cisneros; and economics and public policy professor Robert Reich, who served in both the Ford and Carter administrations and would be named Secretary of Labor by Clinton. After participating at Little Rock, I became known nationally as a business leader with special expertise in the world of media and broadcasting.

Many have said that few U.S. presidents could have absorbed all the information that was presented at the economic summit, but that was Clinton's unique capability and style, for which he was also often criticized. Clinton has a consultative leadership style, meaning he would attempt to gather all the best minds on a subject, listen and absorb their knowledge. Assembling global experts often took a good deal of time, as did his assimilation of their input and his subsequent decisions, given his new and thorough, understanding of complex problems.

That sounds like a process that would lead to an excellent outcome, but there are often trade-offs for good leadership decision making methods. Those who gather the best and the brightest, which takes a long time, are often considered slow and ineffectual. Other leaders try to bring all parties to consensus on a path forward, only to be considered indecisive and not in charge. Or some try what the Trump administration has done and shoot from the hip and be considered powerful, confident, and in charge by some, and often just plain wrong by many others.

Personally, I had been mightily impressed with the willingness of Clinton to call together, and participate in, such an exhaustive review of the country's economic status relative to a whole variety of industries.

After the Clinton inauguration, I began to receive calls from the White House Office of Personnel. Apparently, my background was viewed as a possible fit for several administration job openings. Eventually, the calls focused in on a position on the board of directors of the Corporation for Public Broadcasting (CPB). The CPB is the unique, non-profit steward of government funds used to ensure the continued access, of 99 percent of Americans, to non-commercial, high-quality broadcast content. The CPB distributes its Federal funding to more than 1,600 public radio and television stations nationwide that most people know as NPR and PBS.

The suggestion was flattering to say the least, but I was still very engaged in the life insurance company and had just secured that contract to provide life insurance to all California State University employees. I turned down the White House offer. In hindsight, I find that as difficult to believe as it is to type the words for others to read.

A new vision for my future began to take shape because of my exposure to the work of not-for-profit organizations and the movers and shakers, if you will. During my last year in the insurance business, I began to think seriously about what early retirement could mean, with the hopes that I could find ways to "give back" to the community and the state that had welcomed me and provided the education and business climate that allowed my entrepreneurial spirit to thrive. In 1994 I sold my half of the insurance business to Manny and began a new chapter of my life.

Fortunately, the White House Office of Personnel called again about a year later. Since I had made the decision to leave the partnership with Manny, I was all in this time. Little did I know what I was in for. The personnel office had their own vetting process, which was as detailed as could be imagined. At the same time, the FBI carried out their own investigation into my background. Any friend, neighbor, or former business associate was apt to receive a call from the White House or the FBI. That part of the process was sometimes humorous. When close friend Andy Camacho got a call from the FBI, he put them on hold, called me from another line to ask, "Frank, are you in some kind of trouble, man? I've got the FBI on another line, and they want to talk to me about you!"

After my next-door neighbor completed an unannounced and in-person inquiry from an FBI agent, he came over to my house and asked me if I was "some kind of drug dealer or something."

Years later I was able to help colleagues Bruce Ramer and Professor Ernie Wilson through the same intimidating process. Bruce and Ernie both went on to serve as board members and chairmen of the Corporation for Public Broadcasting for several years.

As for the White House questioning, here are just a few of the 53 questions that candidates were (and I think still are) expected to answer in detail and in writing, if an individual is to continue in the appointment or nomination process. The answers to the 53 questions are in addition to providing all personal and family names, dates, and five years of tax returns, etc.

- List all positions held as an officer, director, trustee, partner, proprietor, agent, representative, or consultant of any corporation, company, firm partnership, or other business enterprise, educational, or other institution.
- List all scholarship, fellowships, honorary degrees, honorary society memberships, military medals, and any other special recognitions for outstanding service or achievement.
- List the titles, publishers, and dates of books, articles, reports, or other published materials that you have written.
- Provide the committee with two copies of any formal speeches you have delivered during the last five years that you have copies of on topics relevant to the position for which you have been nominated.
- Do you know why you were chosen for this nomination by the president?
- Will you sever all connections with your present employers, business firms, business associations, or business organizations if you are confirmed by the Senate?
- Describe all financial arrangements, deferred compensation agreements, and other continuing dealings with business associates, clients, or customers.
- Please discuss your philosophical views on the role of government. Include a discussion of when you believe the government should involve itself in the private sector, when should society's problems be left to the private sector, and what standards should be used to determine when a government program is no longer necessary.

Did I mention that the six-year appointments to the board of directors of the Corporation for Public Broadcasting are unpaid appointments?

A CPB directorship was interesting to me because, since the position had been mentioned to me a year or so earlier, I had been comparing and contrasting the content of commercial media with the programming offered by my local public broadcasting television and radio stations. With each succeeding day, it seemed that the network news was becoming courser and courser; if it bleeds it leads. Every top story was about murders, high-speed chases, etc.

That shift coincided with the introduction of the mini-cam and police scanners. With these new lightweight and less expensive cameras and the ability to listen in on police department communications, freelance video crews found a way of profiting from the fact that the network reporters and their camera crews went home at 5 or 6 p.m. Thus, the night and its often-bloody crime scenes provided the content for the non-union, non-journalist freelancers to photograph and sell their film footage to the stations.

Television is, after all, a visual medium with photography at its base, but we were swiftly entering the 24/7 news cycle, which demanded watered down reporting and precious little space for investigative journalism. The shift in what constituted "news" back then is not unlike the way cell phone videos capture events that can be posted to television stations for immediate broadcast, making every cell phone owner a journalist.

I began to grapple with the realization that it had been an awfully long time since I had been involved with news reporting where I could teach, and I didn't have to sensationalize. I was gravitating more and more often to non-commercial programming and its relevant stories. Hell, the only things that the networks are in business for are ratings and profit. That fact was made clear to me during my 1997 service on the Gore Commission, which I described in the prologue of this book. Whereas my appreciation of public broadcasting was broadened when I was in Washington for interviews. I'd hop in a cab from the Jefferson Hotel to Capitol Hill and every single cab driver was listening to National Public Radio (NPR).

I'd ask them, "What do you like about this news?" A common response was, "It's very balanced. They cover the Middle East very well." My point is that people from countries where the press is likely suppressed, and where propaganda rules, were the very same folks who especially appreciate unbiased, thorough, and relevant reporting.

I began to believe that as a board member of the CPB, I could influence policy and support the balanced and in-depth reporting that I had been able to do decades earlier in Los Angeles, and that public broadcasting stations were, and still are, providing across the entire country.

I did serve on the board of directors of the Corporation for Public Broadcasting for 13 exciting years, starting in 1994. For two of those years, I served as vice chair to Diane Divers Blair, the University of Arkansas political science professor and best friend of First Lady Hillary Rodham Clinton. Becoming a friend and colleague of Diane's was one of the highlights of my service to CPB. Her untimely death was a huge loss. The University of Arkansas held a memorial service for Diane. Along with Hillary and Bill Clinton, I was asked to contribute a eulogy. Later, as chair of CPB I was able to lead a motion to name the conference room in our Washington, D.C., offices, in Diane's honor.

Greeting First Lady Hillary Clinton at Diane Blair's memorial

For me, it was very thrilling to work in the center of power—I got to see how the huge public system of radio and television stations benefits the entire country. But the best was the opportunity to be a part of some programs that, in a very up close and personal way, increased American access to quality journalism and exposure to high-quality programming, while educating and illuminating the minority experience.

Political/Legislative/Funding Support

As alluded to in the prologue of this book, funding from CPB made a huge difference in the lives of Native American peoples in Arizona. Although not through radio or television programming, the impact of CPB's funding was perhaps more profound, and the reason Republican Senator John McCain always supported CPB funding in Senate appropriation bills.

Arizona's Native American population of Navajo and Hopi people suffered without really any form of modern communication equipment. The Hopi live at the top of the mesa and the Navajo live at its base. In our discussions with them, I learned that the two people do not like each other much, so I'm proud we were able to agree on a mutually beneficial solution.

When driving east from Flagstaff, Arizona, you enter the huge reservation lands. Perhaps not immediately, but ultimately you note the absence of telephone lines, cell towers, radio transmitters, and cable lines scarring the Arizona desert vistas around the Four Corners area. But the unspoiled beauty of the landscape contradicted the desperation faced by the inhabitants, especially those who needed emergency healthcare. For example, a young Hopi woman who had gone into labor, and her husband, might have driven 50 or 100 miles to the nearest health clinic, only to find that the only doctor in the territory had visited patients earlier in the day and had left some hours earlier. Readers can conjure up hundreds of similarly frightening circumstances that might be the result of having no modern forms of communication. I dare admit that my family members and business colleagues would be lost without our cellphone connections.

While I was on its board, CPB allocated sufficient funds to construct a low-power frequency radio station, housed in the community center, on the Navajo and the Hopi reservations, with a broadcast reach of about 40 to 50 miles in all directions. Families could use the station to connect with each other and with emergency services. So, in the case of the young expectant mother, prior to setting out for the long drive to the medical clinic, her husband can now call the station and let the operator know that he and his wife are heading out for the clinic. The attendant can announce the situation on the radio (that be heard in nearly every household and business in the territory). The reservation doctor, in turn, learning when the young couple has left home and approximately how long it will take them to arrive at the clinic can head for the clinic to meet the couple and deliver their child into a more connected, and safer world. Along the way tribal members can contact the station and provide an update to the travel time, as they view the pregnant couple and/or the doctor driving past their house or business. In emergency cases like this and others, the regular programming will be interrupted, much like an Amber Alert or a fire warning interrupts television and/or radio broadcasts in other parts of the country.

Once in operation, the low-power transmission also became a public service vehicle in more general terms. While the locals provide their own programming, station operators can break up that programming during the day to cover a sporting event at the high school or provide on-air counseling on diabetes, alcohol, and drug addiction.

Listeners can call in anonymously with all kinds of medical questions and find out about services that might be available to them. They produce half-hour long talk shows with medical professionals discussing prevention strategies and effective disease management guidelines, for example. I've heard people call in and describe their problems with alcohol or anger issues. It seemed clear to me that prior to this station there was a near complete inability to reach out to, or to be sought out by professional assistance. Thus, the anonymity factor is very important when accessing needed help and services, perhaps for the first time.

Because of these services to many of his constituents, Senator John McCain never failed to exercise his influence in support of CPB since the system was installed in Arizona. Indeed, in 2004, as chairman of the Senate Committee on Commerce, Science, and Transportation, Senator McCain was able to push a bill through Congress that reauthorized CPB for several years. He did this with the help of a fellow Republican and a grateful Senator Trent Lott of Mississippi, who had this to say about public broadcasting service in his state:

> "I do not want to miss an opportunity to recognize the achievements of Mississippi Public Broadcasting. My home state's public broadcasting network does an excellent job of serving the people of Mississippi, and I appreciate the good that they do. I have spoken to several of the witnesses here today who know personally of the challenges that must be met in running quality public radio and television stations. The reauthorization of the Corporation for Public Broadcasting is a key way in which we can continue to help our state and local public broadcasting systems, and I look forward to the testimony today for the guidance it will provide in this process."

Mississippi has utilized the state's public television stations to enhance and modernize their public education system. Mississippi Educational Television (ETV) hit the airwaves in 1970. Mississippi was the first state to complete the conversion to digital technology from analog transmission. In 2003, ETV was merged with Mississippi Public Radio and formed Mississippi Public Broadcasting. The state's cutting-edge educational resources for teachers and students, award-winning productions, and acclaimed emergency response operation play a vital role in the lives of educators, students, parents, and caregivers. Mississippi eLearning for Educators, delivered online by Mississippi Public Broadcasting, increases teachers' content knowledge, shares best teaching practices, all to the benefit of student learning.

I worry about the future of public broadcasting in the United States should we lose powerful supporters in Congress.

The cynical side of me, and, yes, I do have a cynical side, worries that a lack of unbiased, national, and international journalism available to parts of rural America might play to the benefit of some political persuasions. But as of this writing, CPB and its funding mechanism for the public television and radio stations across America remains alive and well.

Another political supporter has been Congresswoman Nancy Pelosi. Due to her hard work in the 1980s, Congress created and passed legislation requiring an annual budget for five minority consortia. Every year support is assured for these groups—Native Americans, African Americans, Asian Americans, Latinos, and Hawaiian/Pacific Islanders. CPB monies are used to hire producers to develop shows with the intent to be picked up by PBS. If a producer is awarded this seed money, there was a good chance that the program will make it to the PBS line-up. The call for proposals goes out through Latino Public Broadcasting in Los Angeles, Asian Public Broadcasting in San Francisco, and Native American in Nebraska, etc. Each group receives about $1 million for producers to submit program ideas. The Corporation for Public Broadcasting provides a portion of the funding, with the understanding that the show, series, or documentary will likely air on PBS.

When Congress passed the Public Broadcasting Act of 1967, it was understood that the mission was to offer alternative and enlightened content for the underserved. Some decades later, many complaints were aimed at the heads of National Public Radio (NPR) and Public Broadcasting Service (PBS). The concern was that programming was not living up to its promise. With that language, a mechanism needed to be in place to showcase minority-produced content. Permanent funding for the five minority consortia did just that.

A Crisis at CPB

During my first 10 years on the board of the Corporation for Public Broadcasting, the political interplay among directors had been pretty good. It was common for board members to concern themselves more with the mission of public broadcasting as an alternative to the commercial world rather than to political agendas. Unfortunately, a big deviation developed with President George W. Bush's election in 2000 and with the new people he appointed to the board. They were taking on a more heightened political point of view. It became a serious problem when Ken Tomlinson became chair in 2004. Ken made it a point to declare that PBS was "too liberal." He was vociferous in making the point.

By 2002, President George W. Bush had appointed a majority of conservative board members, although not all were as vocal as Ken. He was constantly complaining to NPR and PBS that they needed to be "much more, fair and balanced" in their broadcasting and programming. He began pushing for conservative type programming and wanted to obtain funding for those types of shows.

These leadership shifts don't take place in a vacuum. At the time, you had the likes of Rush Limbaugh and Michael Savage and the airwaves were full of right-wing commercial radio and television programming. Whereas, the key person on air at the time on public broadcasting was Bill Moyers. He produced a lot of different shows, and it was clear to see that he had taken on the conservative establishment. Ken Tomlinson thought that PBS news shows were too slanted toward the liberal perspective, despite study after study that showed that Americans respected public broadcasting and noted the unbiased and in-depth coverage of news. Ken did not see it that way.

A big problem arose when Ken began taking a lot of action behind the scenes and not informing the other board members, including me, his vice chair. The rest of us were in the dark until the *New York Times* reported in May 2004 that Ken had hired conservative consultants to analyze some shows on public broadcasting. Ken put them on a retainer and had them literally count any "too liberal" perspectives portrayed on shows like *Nova*, *Nightly News*, and *The MacNeil/Lehrer Report*. After the *Times*' article, a good deal was being written describing how Ken had overstepped his bounds. Since CPB is funded with public monies, its board of directors acts as a steward of those funds and has what is called a fiduciary responsibility that money be spent to further the mission of this quasi government agency.

Someone went to Congress and said that Ken was taking a lot of actions and committing CPB funds without the knowledge of the board of directors. I was interviewed under oath about what I knew about Ken's actions. Evidently, CPB President Kathleen Cox would ask Ken if these expenses had been approved by the board, and his response was, "Don't worry, I'll get board approval." Once all of this was reported on, it came out that Ken was also funneling money into a conservative show without consulting with his fellow directors. He had actually begun hiring people for that show when someone leaked his actions to the *Los Angeles Times*. That prompted an extensive investigation by the Inspector General Ken Konz.

The conclusion of the board of directors was that it was best for Tomlinson to leave. In a closed-door session, I took the lead describing our situation as a true crisis. "Yes, we have differences of opinion on this situation," I told the board members, "but if we don't ask Ken to leave and this thing blows up in a negative way and along political lines, Congress could decide to defund public broadcasting and that will be on our watch." In other words, I was trying to convey that the problem was bigger than all of us. My suggestion is that we let Ken go."

If we had decided to create a highly partisan fight, it could have meant the end of public broadcasting, given the angry, conservative mood of several congressional representatives. And it could have been quite a battle among the CPB board members; one of the directors was married to a former aide to Trent Lott (then Senate Majority Whip), and Ken himself had a close relationship with Karl Rove (then White House Deputy Chief of Staff).

Two fellow board members, Beth Courtney and Ernie Wilson, were with me at the Jefferson Hotel the night before the full board met in our D.C. offices. I explained to them my strategy to gain a consensus from the board members. The next morning, the board members agreed unanimously; Ken Tomlinson resigned. Not to be overly dramatic, but if you were to ask either Beth or Ernie today, I think they would probably tell you that Frank Cruz saved public broadcasting at that meeting.

While serving on a board, or even in high level management positions, you must establish yourself as a great listener first. And when you do contribute to a topic, you must convey your ideas in a very, well-thought out manner. Top managers and directors must display an understanding of tactical matters, but always in the context of the big picture—what the impact of any action will have vis a vi the mission of the organization. Effective top managers and directors try to visualize a particular action by their organization in such detail that unintended consequences can be brought to light. This conceptual ability is critical because business people and shareholders will accept risk, but they don't like surprise endings. I have often wished that our government representatives made decisions based less on political expediency and more on a thorough vetting of the impact of a course of action.

CPB board members from left, Katharine Anderson, Ken Tomlinson, Heidi Schulman, Ernie Wilson, Christi Carpenter, Rita Jean Butterworth and chairman Frank Cruz

History Making Programming

American Family was the first Latino drama to air on commercial or public broadcasting, and, one of those once-in-a-lifetime opportunities.

One morning in 2002, I sat down at my kitchen table with a cup of coffee and the *Los Angeles Times*, as I do most every day. That day I read in the Calendar section that CBS-TV had made its selection of programs for the fall season. CBS had a series of very good offerings, and the article listed the television shows the network neglected to include. One was *American Family: Journey of Dreams*. It took me about two minutes to find CBS Chief Executive Officer Les Moonves' telephone number, which I had because he and I had served together on the Gore Commission. I explained to Les that I was chair of the CPB board and that I had read that morning that his network had rejected *American Family*. I asked, "What are the chances that PBS could take it over?"

Les explained that his people in New York had made the selections, "but if you're interested in that property, I can put you in contact with some people and you can have it." All CBS would require is that PBS give the network credit for the first episode that was already "in the can."

That was an amazing gift to public television! Pilot productions for television shows are very expensive because all the locations, props, talent, and technical people must be assembled. If a show is picked up by the network, those initial costs can be spread out over the season. So here we had the award-winning Latino creator and executive producer team of Gregory Nava and Barbara Martínez Jitner with acclaimed cast members Edward James Olmos, Raquel Welch, Esai Morales, and Sonia Braga in a relevant, true-to-life drama filmed in East Los Angeles about residents of East Los Angeles.

I called CPB President and Executive Director Bob Coonrod and explained what I had just read and my conversation with Les. He agreed it would be great for our mission if we wanted to broaden the public broadcasting audience to have programming of interest to Latinos. Bob said, "I'll call Pat Mitchell (who was the first woman president and CEO of PBS) and tell her that and PBS can provide some funding as well." They got in contact with Gregory Nava, who said, "Absolutely!"

CPB contributed $15 million, and PBS put in a comparable amount to fund the series. *American Family* was so well received that we funded a second season. If you ask me, Eddie, or Greg, I think we would all agree it was one of our proudest moments to offer the first and, as yet, the only Latino dramatic series for television in the English language. And the high Nielsen ratings didn't hurt either. Who would have guessed? It is a story about a barber and ex-GI whose wife had passed away. He was raising his children in East Los Angeles with some help from his eccentric sister, and it was shot entirely on location in the barrio!

American Family *cast & crew recognized by National Hispanic Foundation for the Arts*

Two other accomplishments I'm very proud of involve kids' programming. We hit a home run in a partnership with Scholastic. In support of its series of iconic children's books, the company produced a 65-episode adaptation of *Clifford, the Big Red Dog*, which PBS aired for three years beginning while I was chair in 2000. Popular actor John Ritter was the original voice of Clifford. The life lesson messaging for children was so popular that a 39-episode prequel series was created around Clifford's puppyhood, which ran until February

Congratulating Esai Morales at the award ceremony

2006. I understand that there is a new Clifford series set for the fall of 2019 for Amazon Prime Video.

The educational animated series aimed at the 5 to 9 age range, *Maya & Miguel,* met the one criterion for children's television on PBS—education first, then entertainment. The series was produced by Scholastic Studios with animation by Starburst and Yeson animation studios. The five seasons and 65 episodes of *Maya & Miguel* started with the fall line-up in 2004 and ran through October of 2007. The lives and escapades of preteen twins Maya and Miguel Santos combine Spanish dialogue in the English version. In its efforts to promote multiculturalism, Scholastic found ways to inject various traditional holiday activities into the episodes and in the numerous books published based on the television program.

KCET, the public television station in Los Angeles, produced *Niños en Casas* and *A Place of Our Own* in 2005 and 2006. Although filmed on the West Coast, their appeal was national because the shows were aimed uniquely at the caregivers of children. Both were funded by ARCO's foundation. Unlike *Clifford* and *Maya & Miguel*, that were both produced at WGBH in Boston, the success of the KCET productions proved to many in the industry that there was life west of the Hudson River.

I also presided over the CPB board during one of our nation's worst tragedies. WNET-TV on 39th Street in lower Manhattan became the media hub for all networks and press outlets around the world that rushed to New York City on September 11, 2001. Unlike other commercial stations, WNET's proximity to the fallen twin towers made it the unlikely production facility for even our major networks that were headquartered way up by Central Park. WNET President Bob Baker recognized the need to offer access to its studios, equipment, and hook ups to all media outlets. The Corporation for Public Broadcasting had been able to support the world's press coverage by allocating reserve funding to WNET to cover its emergency expenses.

Sadly, the proverbial battles return every so many years. Presidents can present a first pass budget to Congress, that excludes a line item for CPB. It is, however, fortunate that a good cadre of Democrats and Republicans understand the value that public broadcasting brings to their constituents. Folks like U.S. Senator Thad Cochran of Mississippi have supported CPB for the same reason South Carolina and Nebraska elected officials do—not so much for the news but because of the value their local public broadcasting stations bring to their state's educational systems. States with difficult-to-serve rural areas can link programming to those classrooms with teachers who have special expertise but happen to work at a school miles and miles away. This type of exchange has proven, time and again, the unique educational value of public broadcasting.

Serving our nation by chairing the Corporation for Public Broadcasting required all my experience as a college history professor, a television reporter, station manager, a network executive, and an entrepreneur. My total of 13 years at CPB were the culmination of what was a perfectly amazing journey from Barrio Hollywood to Washington, D.C.

Future leaders would do well to consider words that have been stated and written in a variety of speeches and documents but are worth remembering and held up as a guide for decision making.

An educated electorate is critical to the health of a democracy. Since public broadcasting brings fair and balanced news and reports to 99 percent of U.S. households, including those remote rural areas, the system is an essential service to the country and should be preserved and enhanced by our governmental representatives.

Similarly, the public broadcasting system represents an amazing opportunity to help educators and school systems around the country provide excellent learning environments regardless of budgeting issues. Communities of less means can optimize points of excellence across districts and within a state system by engaging with the public broadcasting system as Mississippi educators have done.

"Indeed, the American first amendment is probably the most robust expression and enshrinement of the primacy of free speech in an open society," proclaimed 20-year editor of England's *The Guardian* Alan Rusbridger.

The United States founding fathers valued a free press highly enough to guarantee it in the Constitution. More than 200 years later, I don't have a better description of the value of news reporting that is unfettered by commercial interest, such as is offered by NPR and PBS, than their own words:

"Republics . . . derive their strength and vigor from a popular examination into the action of the magistrates."

Benjamin Franklin

Freedom will be "a short-lived possession" unless the people are informed.

Thomas Jefferson

"The liberty of the press is essential to the security of the state."

John Adams

Epilogue

Having finished writing about my adventures as a fatherless, little brown boy from the barrio (from where, by all rights, I should have never emerged) to the halls of Congress, I felt the need to return to those building blocks written about in the introduction to this memoir. I began to ask myself the same question so many others have asked me. How is it that Frank Cruz came to fight for free public access to quality news reporting and ultimately our nation's entire public broadcasting system?

Surely, I have been blessed with a good mind and a work ethic acquired from my mother. But the process of recounting events of the last 75 years has convinced me that nurturing and relying on those core values became the foundation on which I have been able to build a life around my passion to provide knowledge to, and about, the Latino community. I began to wonder if the use of that ancient pyramid model could be expanded to ultimately create a kind of capstone, on a life of consequence, and to the experiment that is our democracy.

Over the last 20 years or so, I have been recommending this

optimistic outlook to young men and women and business professionals of all ethnicities at every opportunity. Whether they be scientists, educators, journalists, entertainers, or entrepreneurs, with the right combination of self-esteem, global vision, stable family dynamic, valuable experience, relevant education, asset accumulation, and openness to new ideas and opportunities, any of us can give more than we have taken from this life.

In other words, from the vantage point of looking back on our lives, will we be able to say we left the world a kinder place, its inhabitants a little wiser, and civilization in general more sustainable? Because of the qualities and values that I relied on to transition from one career to another, I can respond with an emphatic "yes" to each of those three questions.

The legacy path I've taken has been to become an active contributor to not-for-profit boards of directors within California, the state that has provided me so many opportunities. So, if one wants to characterize my work since leaving the Corporation for Public Broadcasting, I guess "paying it forward" or "giving back" would be apt descriptions.

Serving the community as a director on numerous boards of directors

University of Southern California Trustee

As of this writing, I have been on the board of trustees at my alma mater the University of Southern California (USC), for 18 years. The board has shepherded the school's transition from an expensive, mostly white, party school for athletes and their adoring fans, to a world-class educational institution.

Just in terms of improving the ethnic diversity of student enrollment, I can offer my own personal observation. When I earned my undergraduate degree in history at USC in 1966, I was one of nine Latinos among that graduating class. That dismal statistic must be contrasted with USC's overall enrollment during school year 2017/2018 that included 6,415 students who self-identified as Hispanic.

The student body composition began to change dramatically in 1984 when my dear friend from East Los Angeles College Ed Zapanta became the first Latino trustee of the university. Not long after, Monica Lozano was added to the board and, in 1999, I was the third Latino to join USC's board of trustees. Carmen Nava and Oscar Muñoz are the fourth and fifth Hispanics to become trustees in 2016 and 2018, respectively.

Ed Zapanta, Manny Sánchez, and George Pla founded the Mexican American Alumnae Association at USC in the early 1970s. It became the largest and best known of such groups across the country and the envy of many Chicanos at other universities. I was a television news reporter at the time and served as emcee for many of its fundraising dinners between 1972 and 1975. Raul Vargas served as the association's executive director for many years. Over the next ten years, Raul's successor Domenika Lynch greatly increased the endowment and the scholarships for Latino students. This combination of a strong alumnae group, trustee Zapanta, and then President

John R. Hubbard (1970 to 1980), who believed in Latino issues, literally began to change the face of USC.

Enjoying a USC/Notre Dame game with my best friend and Pulitzer Prize-winning journalist Frank del Olmo

Just as dramatic is the improvement in the academic ranking of incoming students over the past decade. As trustees, we receive annual reports from Vice President of Admissions and Planning Kathryn Harrington on the makeup of the student population.

In 2005, Kathryn reported that USC's incoming freshmen class surpassed UCLA's in any combination of grade point averages and SAT scores. In 2006, USC's incoming freshman class came from every state in the United States except Wyoming, and those new students were equally qualified with students newly-enrolled at California Institute of Technology (Cal Tech) by the same academic measures. And the 2018/2019 incoming freshman class at USC is more qualified by grade point average and SAT scores than those students entering Stanford. For the second year in a row, they've come to USC from all 50 United States, and nearly 20 percent arrived from the East Coast.

I began my first full year as a trustee in 2000. I must admit to being more than a little in awe of the team of talented individuals from a wide range of industries with whom I would be serving as a trustee. The make-up of the board is no less impressive today:

- from the media is Frederick Ryan, president and CEO of the *Washington Post*;
- from industry is Ronald Sugar, chair emeritus of Northrup Grumman;
- from entertainment is Steven Spielberg, chair of Amblin Partners;
- a variety of philanthropists including Wallis Annenberg and Ed Roski
- from sports is Jeanie Buss, owner of Los Angeles Lakers; and Peter Ueberroth, former baseball commissioner and head of the 1984 Olympics host committee;
- from transportation is Oscar Munoz, CEO of United Airlines;
- from commercial real estate development is Rick Caruso;
- from pharmaceuticals is Gavin Herbert, founder of Allergan;
- from big oil is Richard Stegemeir, chair emeritus Unocal Corporation;
- from residential real estate development is J. Douglas Pardee, chair emeritus of Pardee Construction;
- from high tech is Andrew Viterbi, co-founder of Qualcomm.

The full list of distinguished individuals who serve as USC trustees bring a wide range of expertise and diverse perspectives to guide the institution.

A board of directors, or in this case a board of trustees, is responsible for setting the overarching direction or the mission for an organization. In pursuit of those goals, the board members recruit and hire the top manager, be it the CEO in corporations or the president in academia. That individual is entrusted with hiring and grooming the next level of administrators who, with their employees and faculty, will carry out the trustees' vision for the organization. Although university presidents across the country have an average tenure of three to four years, since USC's doors opened in 1880, the school has only had 11 presidents.

Even with the most effective individuals in charge, dramatic shifts in a large institution don't come easy. In 1991, USC found itself in a critical position. The university needed a new president and the board of trustees had reached consensus that USC should become a world-class institution. A new leader had to be found who would drive the necessary changes.

Fortunately, eminent scholar and acclaimed leadership author and consultant Warren Bennis was a professor at USC at the time. Warren brought Steve Sample to the attention of the other board members. Sample had been president of the State University of New York at Buffalo, Illinois State University, and the University of Nebraska.

Sample had already been president of USC for eight years when I was asked to join the board of trustees. But the stories of his hiring interviews had become something of legend.

The focus of questioning centered around two main points: Sample's public university successes versus the absence of private school experience and the board of trustees' goal to shift the culture at USC to that of a world-class educational institution.

Apparently, Steve Sample laid out precisely what was needed to realize the goals. "You can continue to be a jock, football, white, party school, he said. "But if you want to become an eminent institution, here's what you have to do. You'll need to hire transformational faculty at every opportunity, improve the academic strength of incoming freshmen every year, and increase the rigor of the curriculum every semester."

Sample added that he was up for the task, but he warned that tough decisions would need to be made day-by-day, week-by-week, semester-by-semester. He needed to know that the trustees had the courage to stand with him as he changed the culture and the corresponding stature of the university. Sample was appointed president of USC in the 1991/1992 school year. And what a time it was to take the reins of a major Los Angeles institution.

In early March 1991, unarmed African American truck driver Rodney King was severely beaten by four Los Angeles Police Department officers. The attack ensued after a high-speed chase just south of downtown Los Angeles. The horrific beating was caught on video and immediately picked up by all local television stations and went pre-Internet viral via CNN. Tempers flared in South Central Los Angeles and literally erupted on April 29,1992 when the not guilty verdict was reached by the jurors in the criminal trial against the four police officers.

The Los Angeles riots of 1992 claimed the lives of some 60 Angelinos. Two thousand people were injured and 9,500 were arrested for rioting, looting, and arson. At one point, with more than 100 fires burning, the city in flames looked more like Hell than the City of Angels.

I watched from my office in downtown Los Angeles, knowing my twins, Frankie and Vanessa, were both living in dorms on the USC campus. All classes had been cancelled, of course. Although situated at the epicenter of the destruction, the campus was astonishingly untouched.

To say that Los Angeles had been shaken to its core is not overstating the situation. LAPD Chief Darryl Gates submitted his resignation and African American officer Willie Williams was appointed in his place and expected to institute many changes in the department. Five term Mayor Tom Bradley announced soon thereafter that he would not seek re-election. Given this contentious environment, USC's new president was under incredible pressure to move the university out of town, as Pepperdine University had done in 1971 and Loyola Marymount University had followed in 1972.

To President Sample's credit, he resisted the calls to move the campus from the city's core. Hundreds of times he described his vision of Los Angeles becoming a leading force in the Pacific Rim economies and, to that end, USC must remain located in a major metropolis. Sample's passionate declaration was effective. Talk of relocating USC out of town ended.

And Steve Sample's involvement was not only at the strategic level. For several semesters, he and his friend and coach Warren Bennis co-taught a leadership class that was one of the most popular on campus despite its rigor. Those lucky students and everyone else on campus were already seeing those popular lectures play out in real life. We were all getting a major lesson in leadership as we observed Sample's inspirational style while he managed the details of the university's transformation.

During the 2005/06 school year, the university went through a routine accreditation review. That involves a team of outside educators and administrators who review university practices, evaluate student outcomes, and measure the degree to which policies are sound and administered fairly. In addition to several USC schools that have specialized accreditation through related organizations, the university overall is accredited by the Western Association of Schools and Colleges (WASC). The accreditation team may make specific recommendations for improvement that will be expected to have been implemented by the time the next accreditation visit is scheduled. Ultimately, the school is either accredited by WASC or not.

That year, we were fortunate that our accreditation team was led by Derrick Bok. He was a Stanford University graduate who had served two terms as president of Harvard University. After the team was on campus for a few days, Bok called for a meeting with a few of the trustees. He wanted no note takers, no staffers, and none of the other accreditation team present. It was quite unusual for this type of meeting to take place, but those of us who were available sat down with Bok. I imagine some of the trustees were a bit nervous, as was I.

Derrick Bok soon put any anxiety to rest. He said, "I've served on a lot of accreditation teams over the years and, I must say, you have a very unique president. I've never known a university president to take on so many critical initiatives at one time, Oh, they might work toward increasing the quality of the faculty and all that would entail."

"Or they might look at improving the qualifications of incoming students," he continued. "But I have never seen an individual take on all the initiatives that your president has, and the university is achieving all his goals and on his timetable. Or said another way, I've seen colleges move the needle in one direction or another, but I have never seen the needle moved in so many areas at once. And quite remarkably, amid all the changes taking place at USC, President Sample is also liked and respected by all constituent groups—academic senate, students, and alumni—which hastens his accomplishments."

Bok was also complimentary of the makeup of the board of trustees, "Half of the trustees are not USC graduates, and you come from a wonderful mix of industries. We don't see this very often," he added.

Perhaps even more exciting was Bok's assessment of USC's positioning in terms of globalism. Reviewing department by department, school by school, he commented on the very well-prepared curriculum and faculty, which he believed translated to graduates with the all-important global vision required of today's leaders.

As a trustee, I was very proud of the support we had given to President Sample. I think we all believe we were important contributors to the dramatic culture shift and the increased financial strength President Sample would need to accomplish the second phase in the transformation of the university. Sadly, due to failing health Steve Sample had to hand over the reins to another visionary in 2010.

Max Nikias had been a student of Professor Steve Sample years before at State University of New York at Buffalo. Following his mentor to USC, Professor Nikias joined the faculty of the USC Viterbi School of Engineering.

I can testify to the rigor of the year-long search for the president's successor. By Sample's departure in 2010, Max Nikias had already served as second in charge of the campus—provost of USC—for five years. We chose Max Nikias, from among a host of stellar candidates, to be the new president of the University of Southern California.

I had been a trustee by that time for 10 years and was about to witness the transition of the Keck School of Medicine of USC to a genuine medical research institution on par with Harvard, Johns Hopkins, and Stanford. Nikias' first step was to purchase hospitals in the area around USC. Next, the faculty was augmented with brilliant researchers who are also excellent practitioners. Also, during this time, the trustees, along with Nikias, were building the USC endowment to ensure the long-term success of the university.

Today, USC operates more than 40 California hospitals and clinics in Los Angeles, Kern, and Orange Counties; Keck Hospital of USC, a 400-bed, acute care hospital staffed with internationally-known physicians from the Keck School of Medicine; USC Norris Comprehensive Cancer Center and Hospital, a 60-bed facility and one of eight cancer centers designated by the National Cancer Institute; and USC Verdugo Hills Hospital, a 158-bed, community hospital serving the northeast portion of the San Gabriel Valley.

Like any large institution, and USC is the eighth largest employer in Los Angeles County, problems will occur. The university and its students, alumni, and trustees have suffered on many levels when senior officials have failed to uphold the public trust. Personally, I am grateful for the opportunity to be a part of the university's successes and to offer some wisdom, gleaned from my 50 years of experience in academia and the media, when problems do arise.

Indeed, Max Nikias resigned in 2018 amid three painful scandals involving faculty wrongdoing, which the university has viewed as systemic failures for which leadership rightly must accept the brunt of the blame.

Director Irvine Foundation

The story of the Irvine family is one for the history books. I'll try to keep it short. James Irvine and a younger brother escaped the potato famine in Ireland by emigrating to the United States in the mid-1800s. A couple of years later, James followed the gold rush to California and opened a wholesale produce company on Front Street in San Francisco. A successful merchant, James purchased the Rancho San Joaquín and the Rancho Lomas de Santiago for a total of more than 110,000 acres in Southern California. After the 1906 San Francisco earthquake, James moved his family to a portion of that land, to what is now Irvine, California.

James' son, James II, inherited most of his dad's property. He bought out other family members and founded the Irvine Company in 1892. James II had a son, James III, who predeceased his father and died in 1937. It was then that James II started the Irvine Foundation to honor his son's memory. The endowment was chartered very specifically to benefit Californians and emphatically noted that no public entity was to benefit.

Fast forward to 2001 and 2002, when the foundation was recruiting a new president. The search was focused up in Northern California because, though the family lived in the southern part of the state, the foundation had remained headquartered near the financial hub of California. One of the candidates was President and Executive Vice President Mary Bitterman of KQED, a dual-licensed public television and radio station in San Francisco. I knew Mary well because she had hosted all of the member public broadcasting stations at KQED one year when I chaired CPB. The Irvine Foundation board of directors hired Mary in part because she and the foundation were very local and Bay Area centric. But Mary

Bitterman began to change the Northern California and white male orientation of the Irvine Foundation from the get-go.

Mary added another woman to the board. Molly Munger is the very liberal-minded daughter of Charlie Munger, co-founder of Berkshire Hathaway. Peter Taylor was the first African American and the second Southern Californian to join Molly on the board. We were seeing the early breakup of the Northern Californian control of the Irvine Foundation. Next, Mary asked me to join the board and soon thereafter she invited David "Mas" Masumoto from the Central Valley, to join us.

Thus, the diversity on the board was complete not only from a racial and gender perspective but also geographically.

Mary Bitterman served as board chair for just a year and a half, but her vision that the foundation should serve all of California transformed the Irvine Foundation in every way.

The board searched for a new leader, and we hired Jim Canales. Thus, the democratization of the board really began to take hold. I served on the governance committee that selected new members.

The Irvine Foundation is probably the largest funding source of the arts in California. I was so proud to serve on the board. Another source of pride was that we were able to increase the endowment to $2 billion, which nets between $75 and $100 million each year. We made that happen. Together with the chief investment officer, we balanced out the portfolio completely.

The 12 Irvine Foundation board members serve six-year terms, and only two terms can be served. I brought in Paula Cordeiro, dean of the School of Leadership and Education Sciences at the University of San Diego; Regina Muehlhauser;

and Judge Lydia Villareal, now the current chair of the foundation.

With very diverse board members and a new focus on "where the need is the greatest" throughout the state, the Irvine Foundation was positioned to really make an impact.

In 2004, under the leadership of Jim Canales, the projects we funded also began to change. As board members, we were presented with proposals for projects in Salinas, San Diego, and Riverside. The more diverse board was now transitioning from being focused on supporting philharmonic orchestras and fine art museums to locating poverty communities and funding projects in those areas.

As all major foundations do quite often, we took an assessment of the Irvine Foundation and its relevance to California's needs. We considered the most pressing issues facing the state of California: job related, housing, immigration, education, etc. We decided that we would develop key initiatives around public education, readiness for careers of the future, and voting equity. I am happy to report we developed and funded some novel approaches to each.

As trustees, we wanted to learn what were the most needed careers for the future of California. To do the research, we engaged the consulting firm Bridgespan. Soon thereafter, the consultants reported that our economy was going to need policy people, medical professionals, other health care workers, journalists, and experts in several other fields. The trustees decided that we could fund 16 schools throughout the state, each with a separate career path matched to Bridgespan's data.

For example, after multiple discussions with administrators, parents, and the school board for one high school in

Sacramento, we were able to settle on health care careers as the focal point of their curriculum. In that particular case, all the students were from the barrio. Education Program Director, Annie Stanton, was able to convince the local educators and the California Department of Education that all curriculum could be centered on health-related topics.

As an example of this new focus, a 12-year-old girl told us that because her aunt was a nurse, she had always wanted to be a nurse. So, she and her fellow students in a history class learned about the health issues affecting civilization in different eras; i.e., the impact of malaria on world exploration, the 1918 flu pandemic, the invention of antibiotics, etc. When the same students went to English class, they wrote essays on topics like medical breakthroughs or the spread of disease through refugee camps.

The foundation also funded a media school in Los Angeles. Students had to want to be at the Irvine Foundation supported school. We hired the Stanford Research Institute (SRI) to monitor and analyze student outcomes, such as grades, attendance, and retention. Those data points were important because the results were so positive that we were able to successfully propose the program at the state level. Impressed with SRI's reporting on student outcomes, the State of California appropriated $150 million to the program they dubbed Pathways. For more than 10 to 12 years, the Irvine Foundation has invested $120 million in these schools, including the costs of research and data collection.

The second aspect of our strategic planning process was to go through a reality check in terms of what were the vital needs of the state and how that compared to the focus of our efforts. We found that a key challenge for California was the need for governance reform.

We looked to California Democracy, a group headed by Amy Domínguez-Arms, that dealt with a broad range of governance issues including voting registration and equal representation. Amy was very involved with securing grants in an effort to reach those who don't vote in communities with low voter turnout.

In California, as in most states, we had primary elections with five, six, or eight candidates vying for one spot. The top vote-getting Republican and Democrat candidates then moved on to the general election. California Democracy's research showed that the will of the people would be better served if the top two primary candidates, regardless of political affiliation, moved on to the general election. The Irvine Foundation lobbied for a more representative result of voters' wishes from California primary elections. Passed in 2012, California Senate Bill 28 provided for the two candidates for statewide offices (not federal offices) who receive the most votes, regardless of political party affiliation, to move forward to the general election ballot. Not many know how this change in California governance came about.

I am very proud that I was able to serve on the board of directors of the Irvine Foundation at a time when its very makeup and mission were dramatically changed to truly reflect and serve all of California.

Director Latino Public Broadcasting

Latino Public Broadcasting supports a unique, important, and artistic voice for independent filmmakers whose genius might otherwise go largely unnoticed. To right a wrong or pursue equity where it does not exist, brave individuals must take risks and step up to challenges. In this case, we have

Congresswoman Nancy Pelosi to thank for many things especially Latino Public Broadcasting.

As the few examples I've offered previously attest, the public broadcasting system in the United States is responsible for so much more than news programming, although that is curiously what seems to grab the attention of many politicians. For a more complete assessment, we need only enjoy the high art of the *Masterpiece* series, the in-depth and epic Ken Burns documentaries, the scientific adventures offered by *NOVA* and *Nature*, and a broader world view from *Travel with Rick Steves*.

In addition, public broadcasting's impact on education in the United States goes way beyond *Sesame Street* and *Curious George*. But viewers who don't live in Arizona, Georgia, Louisiana, or Mississippi may be completely unaware how those states have leveraged the capabilities of public broadcasting stations, equipment, and connectivity to put directly into the classrooms some of the most innovative and cost-effective learning techniques teachers and school districts can dream up.

The challenge of public broadcasting's relevancy to our country's increasingly more multicultural population began to surface in the late 1980s. Part of addressing the challenge was, and is, that nearly all new content produced for public broadcasting still originates from just three production studios: WETA in Washington, D.C., WGBH in Boston, and WNET in New York. Precious little programming is being produced in the West. The CPB board members had numerous talks with Congresswoman Pelosi about the treasure trove of diverse artistic talent that found it difficult, if not impossible, to break into that system.

These minority, independent film and television producers explained that they couldn't get their product on the air. The producers also made the significant point that public broadcasting gets government money, but a huge swath of the country does not benefit because a good deal of programming misses the mark when it comes to being relevant to minority groups.

Well, Pelosi really listened and then did her own homework. She initiated movement among her colleagues to first recognize the inequity and to ultimately construct a plan to disperse funds to better serve diverse communities.

Congress conducted hearings, and, in the end, it was decided that out of the annual budget of the Corporation for Public Broadcasting, approximately $5 million would be distributed equally among five-member entities making up the National Minority Consortia (NMC). As a group, the member organizations share the mission to address the need for programming that reflects the growing ethnic and cultural diversity in the United States. The funds are to be used for operating capital and to purchase PBS programs relevant to their viewers.

Each member of the consortia has a home base: Latino Public Broadcasting (LPB) is well situated in Burbank, California; Vision Maker Media (VMM) focuses on Native American issues with office space at the University of Nebraska in Lincoln; the Center for Asian American Media (CAAM) operates from San Francisco, California; Black Public Media (BPM) is located on 126th Street in New York, New York; and Pacific Islanders in Communication operates from Honolulu, Hawaii.

Though each NMC member has a different strategy to leverage its annual CPB grant, with private and other public funding, each puts out an annual call for projects that will be of interest to its viewers. For example, at Latino Public

Broadcasting, we put out a call for compelling documentary concepts from Latino would-be producers. We have one outstanding example that tells the untold individual stories of all the Latino technical personnel behind the iconic George Stevens film *Giant*, that starred Elizabeth Taylor, Rock Hudson, and James Dean.

But I'm getting a little ahead of the story.

Diane Blair was chair of CPB and I was vice chair, when the 2000-2001 renewal for the Latino member of the consortia needed to be decided. The best proposal was put together by Edward James Olmos and his partner Marlena Dermer. In addition to presenting a better plan to address the mission of the consortium, Edward James Olmos' award-winning roles in *Zoot Suit* (the play and the film) and television drama *Miami Vice* had made him a good spokesperson for Latino entertainment. A few months after I completed my second term on the board in 2002, the board members picked Eddie, as I have come to call him, to head up Latino Public Broadcasting (LPB).

I was asked to join the board of directors of Latino Public Broadcasting a few years later and I remain on the LPB board because I think my industry experience, my former role as CPB chair, and my years of reporting on Latino issues make me a valuable contributor.

As an example, at one point, the great documentarian Ken Burns completed a multi-part program on World War II for PBS. Ken's work is always very good and thoughtful. He has often expressed his gratitude for public broadcasting for giving him the latitude that he needs and wants to turn out those blockbusters that air for weeks. However, this program, on the war, failed to mention the fact that, on a percentage basis, Latino soldiers won more Medals of Honor than any other ethnic group of Americans who fought in World War II.

In fact, he didn't really mention the service of Latino men and women as soldiers or defense workers at all.

From the vantage point of our LPB board positions, Eddie and I were able to exert a little pressure. The conversation with PBS President and CEO Paula Kerger went something like this,

> "Paula, you likely don't know that my mother was a widow at age 23 with two young boys to raise by herself in a barrio outside of Tucson, Arizona. She opened a small restaurant with money she had managed to save. My brother and I worked there throughout our childhoods. What I want you and Ken to know is that out in front of Mom's café the most vicious fights I ever saw often took place in the late evenings.
>
> I quickly learned the men were veterans of World War II and recently-returned soldiers from the Korean Conflict. The two groups would battle it out, each side boasting more medals, more bravery, and more dramatic war stories. Paula, there is a story here and Ken needs to explore it before he wraps up an incomplete chronicle of U.S. sacrifice in World War II."

Perhaps as a result of my appeal to Paula and the major campaign led by Professor Maggie Rivas-Rodriguez at University of Texas at Austin, Latino film producer Hector Galán, from Texas, was hired to produce an entire segment on the involvement of Latinos in World War II. Ken Burns agreed to insert the Latino chapter into his documentary. Ken Burns is so highly regarded as a PBS documentarian that he is rarely, if ever, questioned about his storytelling. But leaders must accept as an important aspect of their responsibilities, the risk of speaking up, even to the experts.

Latino Public Broadcasting is well staffed with experienced professionals and led by Sandie Pedlow, a former PBS senior program officer. We pick three or four productions and allocate roughly $40 to $50 thousand each and often allow the producers three to four years to complete their projects. The producers will undoubtedly require a good deal more funding than what we can provide, but with ours as seed money and with the strong possibility that PBS will air the final documentary, drama, or mystery, additional grant requests are viewed with greater legitimacy.

The inspector general and others conduct a thorough audit of each consortia member. The auditors' questions might include: "We see in 2015 you selected five shows to be produced. Please tell us where those projects are now vis a vis their contracts." Each consortia member group must prove they are good stewards of the CPB annual grants.

Over the past several years, NMC members have provided hundreds of hours of culturally diverse programs to PBS, made possible by those annual grants from the Corporation for Public Broadcasting budget. Thank you, Congresswoman Nancy Pelosi and Congresswoman Lucille Roybal-Allard, who as a member of the influential Appropriations Committee, makes sure funding for CPB and the NMC continues.

In just the five years between 2009 and 2014, Latino Public Broadcasting programs have won 85 awards, including the prestigious George Foster Peabody Award, two Emmys, two Imagen Awards, and the Sundance Film Festival Award for Best Director, Documentary. Latino Public Broadcasting has been the recipient of the Norman Lear Legacy Award and the National Council of La Raza (NCLR) Alma Award for Special Achievement—Year in Documentaries.

Ahead of My Time, I Guess

Years ago, when I participated in, then President-elect, Bill Clinton's Little Rock Economic Summit, I had the pleasure of having some great conversations with then Secretary of Labor, now UC Berkeley professor, Robert Reich. In one of those conversations, almost like a lecture, he explained to me that in the future young people will need to expect to have three or four distinct careers in their working lives. He was very clear that he was not talking about moving up the ladder from one department to another in the same company but completely distinct industries and job requirements.

I didn't tell him then, but I have often thought about his words since. He didn't realize he was talking to someone who had already lived that life.

However, I should take the opportunity here to directly address young people who may be frightened by the idea of changing careers, industries, and or altering lifetime goals. I'll admit it sounds expensive and like a lot of time wasted in unsatisfying jobs. But I can share that throughout my long working life I have met hundreds of people who are working "in the zone" as some social scientists might say. These folks love the work they are doing and find it so rewarding that they rarely refer to it as "work." So, I've questioned many of them about how they landed in that field.

Surprisingly, very few started out in those types of jobs or even in those industries. You could say that they "hadn't known, what they didn't know," when it came to articulate their life's purpose. But it seems to me, that very often when a person begins, with a high degree of curiosity, to consider all that he or she doesn't know, that a path begins to open toward a series of careers that in some way relate to a developing passion, a defining purpose. Renown champion of ethical conduct and character education Michael Josephson would call such an outcome as living a worthy life.

In my case, I certainly didn't start out in the barrio being driven by a passion to correct the historical record of Hispanics. I can say that over time however, I began to be propelled by an attraction to stretching my knowledge and capabilities combined with a desire to honor my mother's entrepreneurial spirit. This brings up the important distinction between motivation and core values.

To be motivated by the hard-working example my mother set for me as a young boy, or the success stories of business executives I rubbed shoulders with during my life, really has little to do with the thread that ultimately linked my own ventures to the core value of education. As a teacher, a reporter, a television network executive, and as a trustee to various non-profit organizations, I have found my niche, my purpose.

In the process of avidly pursuing five very distinct careers, I have been thrilled and fulfilled by each and wouldn't have had it any other way. It's exciting to me that future generations will, as a matter of the labor market structure, have the same wonderful opportunities for exploration and mastery in a variety of endeavors.

To you who have chosen to read my memoir, please keep in mind that any success I have achieved arose Straight out of Barrio Hollywood.

Acknowledgements

First and foremost, I want to thank my co-author, Rita Soza, without whom this book would not exist. It was Rita who suggested that I consider writing my memoir and for that I am grateful. She spent many hours with me capturing my voice and thoughts.

I also want to thank my many friends and colleagues who over the years have suggested that I write my story. Especially encouraging were friends Rubén Martinez, Anita Cano, David Hayes Bautista, and Rudy Acuña.

Rita and I both owe a special thanks to Professor Felix Gutiérrez whose artful and scholarly approach to the material, provided helpful comments and revisions to strengthen the book. Similarly, we appreciate Katharine Diaz for her sensitive and thorough editing of the manuscript.

I want to acknowledge the KVEA-TV and Telemundo founding pioneers, especially Joe Wallach and Carmen Hensch, who urged me to document the real story of how Telemundo began. We had a lot of fun recalling those days.

So many family members and friends in Barrio Hollywood of Tucson, Arizona, so lovingly and carefully made this book a reality. In particular, the encouragement from Gloria Reynaga, Ernesto Portillo, Sr., and my sister-in-law, Hortencia Cruz, was so very much appreciated.

My many friends and colleagues at the University of Southern California, The James Irvine Foundation, and Latino Public Broadcasting, have enriched my life and helped me in unique ways, more than they will ever know.

Rita and I reserve a special thank you to Pamela Meistrell who designed the book cover and captured my life's journey by restoring old photographs.

Bonnie Cruz, my lovely wife and the mother of our children, was as important to getting this book completed as I was. She read early drafts and reminded me of key events and individuals in my life. And I owe a special thanks to our incredibly successful and very busy children Heather, Frankie, and Vanessa who also made time to read drafts of the book. In the end, I suppose this work was taken on, in large part, for the amusement of our wonderful grandchildren Mays, Sabina and Anais who have brought so much joy to our lives.

Frank H. Cruz

2017 Family vacation in Hawaii (left to right) Vanessa Cruz and son Mays, Alia Cruz and daughter Sabina, Frank R. Cruz and daughter Anais, me and wife Bonnie, Michael Nitabach and wife Heather Cruz

Working as Frank's co-author I have learned so much, especially that humility and graciousness still exist among the most accomplished. He has inspired me to increase those qualities in my everyday life.

Motion picture publicity icon Murray Weissman taught me how to write and many division execs at Emerson Electric Co. gave me the opportunity to hone my skills by communicating on their behalf.

I am ever grateful to my husband Geoff Soza, my mother Evelyn Joiner, and my daughter and son-in-law, Sunny Elizabeth and Douglas Grean for whom, and from whom, I gather the love and courage to pursue inspiring projects.

Rita Joiner Soza

Index